First Edition 2018

How to Be an MVP in Life:
Lessons in Living and Leading from Sports & Tech MVPs

David P. Lundell

How to Be an MVP in Life, by David P. Lundell

First Edition 2018

Edited by Levi Melton
Cover Image by istock.com/BrianAJackson
Cover Design by Laura Boyle

To two of the MVPs in my life:
My mother, Gail, and my father, Don.

Till We Meet Again,

David

Photo and Art Credits:
By Lance Cpl. Ethan Hoaldridge: Steve Young, Feb 10, 2006
Public Domain
https://commons.wikimedia.org/wiki/File:Steve_Young_and_Michael_Irvin.jpg

By benefit1970 - Flickr: Steve Nash and Andre Miller
CC BY 2.0
https://commons.wikimedia.org/w/index.php?curid=18933980

By daveynin from United States: Sidney Crosby and his cup
CC BY 2.0
https://commons.wikimedia.org/w/index.php?curid=59330080

By Arturo Pardavila III from Hoboken, NJ, USA: World Series MVP Ben Zobrist and his new 50th anniversary Chevy Camaro
CC BY 2.0
https://commons.wikimedia.org/w/index.php?curid=52777103

By Whitney & Matt Dellinger from Atlanta, GA, USA: Meeting Dale Murphy at CNN Center
CC BY 2.0
https://commons.wikimedia.org/w/index.php?curid=2904399

By Allyson Lundell: Sketch of Basketball in Motion
Used with Permission

By Allyson Lundell: Sketch of Hockey Puck in Motion
Used with Permission

By Allyson Lundell: Sketch of Baseball in Motion
Used with Permission

By Allyson Lundell: Sketch of Football in Motion
Used with Permission

All Microsoft MVP Photos came from their LinkedIn Pages or MVP Profiles.

Any other photos used were taken by the author or are otherwise credited and used with permission.

Table of Contents

What's Inside?

Inside you will find inspiring stories of five MVPs from Baseball, Basketball, Hockey, and American Football. Along with these, you will also discover amazing stories from 19 people (including me) who are either Microsoft MVPs themselves (and hence are Tech MVPs) or are associated with the Microsoft MVP program. Finally, you will learn what a Microsoft MVP is, how you can be one, and (of course!) *How to Be an MVP in Life!*

Steve Nash
2x MVP

Sid "the Kid" Crosby
2x MVP

Steve Young
2x MVP

Dale Murphy
2x MVP

Hal Hostetler
20-year MVP
Windows, Office
Radio Expert

Jessica Moss
10-Year MVP
Business Intelligence
Author, Speaker

Michael Washington
11-year MVP
Machine Learning Author

Andy Milford
2-year MVP
Remote Desktop
Serial Entrepreneur

Mark Minasi
15-year MVP
Windows, Directory
Author 40+ Books

Brian Desmond
15-year MVP
Identity Management
Youngest MVP

Kathy Jacobs
Former MVP (15 yrs)
PowerPoint & OneNote
Serial Volunteer

Clint Wyckoff
2-year MVP
Cloud & Data Center
Cancer Survivor

Naseem Tuffaha, Sr.
Led MVP Program for
Microsoft **Went Into a Warzone to Teach!**

Jason Brimhall
4-year MVP
SQL Server
Scout Leader and Coach

Octavio Hernandez
Former MVP (6yrs)
.NET Programming
Cuban Expat

Gretchen Mann
Former MVP (5 yrs)
CRM
Accidental IT Career

Joe Kaplan
15-year MVP
Directory & Identity
Author & Speaker

Rob Richardson
4-year MVP
.NET Programming
Hackathons to Benefit Charities

Mike Halsey
7-year MVP
Windows & Devices for IT
Awesome Videos!

Josep Solanes
Former MVP (2 yrs)
Windows Server for SMB
Spanish & Catalan

Pablo Ariel Di Loreto
4-year MVP
Azure and Windows and Devices for IT
Two Category MVP

Rob Prouse
1-year MVP
Programming
13 Million Times Downloaded!

David P Lundell

Part I The MVP & the Accidental meeting of World Series MVP Ben Zobrist

On March 26 of 2018, while on a flight into Dallas-Fort Worth Airport, I was working on this book (at the time I was about 90% of the way done with my first draft). Across the aisle from me was 2016 Major League Baseball World Series MVP Ben Zobrist. Ben is the hero of millions of Chicago Cubs fans, having both ended their 108-year drought and led the Cubs to the promised land of a World Series victory. Even before I recognized him as a professional baseball player and MVP, I observed him helping an older lady maintain her balance as we prepared to disembark. He was courteous, just as all people should be but not all are. He was on his way to Florida for the Cubs' Opening Day game against the Marlins. He had one teammate and a trainer with him. They had to catch a connecting flight, yet he took the time to help this woman. After we deplaned, I introduced myself, described the book I was writing, and asked if I could interview him. He kindly assented, provided I could walk with him to his gate.

1 Ben Zobrist 2016 World Series MVP

David P Lundell

6

Chapter 1: The MVP

The Phoenix Suns of the National Basketball Association (NBA) ended their 2004 season with 29 wins and 53 losses. When they closed their next season in 2005, they stood atop the NBA with 62 wins and only 20 losses – a full three games better than the next best team. They went from one game out of last place in their conference to best team in their conference (and in the whole league) in ONE year (Steve Nash, 2016).

2 Suns Climb to the Top

2004 NBA Standings

Western Conference	W	L	W/L%
Minnesota Timberwolves* (1)	58	24	0.707
San Antonio Spurs* (3)	57	25	0.695
Los Angeles Lakers* (2)	56	26	0.683
Sacramento Kings* (4)	55	27	0.671
Dallas Mavericks* (5)	52	30	0.634
Memphis Grizzlies* (6)	50	32	0.61
Houston Rockets* (7)	45	37	0.549
Denver Nuggets* (8)	43	39	0.524
Utah Jazz (9)	42	40	0.512
Portland Trail Blazers (10)	41	41	0.5
Golden State Warriors (11)	37	45	0.451
Seattle SuperSonics (12)	37	45	0.451
Phoenix Suns (13)	29	53	0.354
Los Angeles Clippers (14)	28	54	0.341

https://www.basketball-reference.com/leagues/NBA_2004_standings.html

2005 NBA Standings

Western Conference	W	L	W/L%
Phoenix Suns* (1)	62	20	0.756
San Antonio Spurs* (2)	59	23	0.72
Dallas Mavericks* (4)	58	24	0.707
Seattle SuperSonics* (3)	52	30	0.634
Houston Rockets* (5)	51	31	0.622
Sacramento Kings* (6)	50	32	0.61
Denver Nuggets* (7)	49	33	0.598
Memphis Grizzlies* (8)	45	37	0.549
Minnesota Timberwolves (9)	44	38	0.537
Los Angeles Clippers (10)	37	45	0.451
Los Angeles Lakers (11)	34	48	0.415
Golden State Warriors (12)	34	48	0.415
Portland Trail Blazers (13)	27	55	0.329
Utah Jazz (14)	26	56	0.317
New Orleans Hornets (15)	18	64	0.22

https://www.basketball-reference.com/leagues/NBA_2005_standings.html

What was the difference?

How does a team go from winning barely more than one third of their games to winning more than three quarters of them in a single year? They added an **MVP** to their team – a Canadian player named Steve Nash.

> "They added an MVP to their team –
> a Canadian player named Steve Nash"

Nash scored only 15.5 points per game, barely half as many points as the league's leading scorer. However, his team went from 94.2 points scored per game to 110.4 points per game (2003-04 Phoenix Suns Roster and Stats, n.d.).

3 Suns Points Per Game Difference

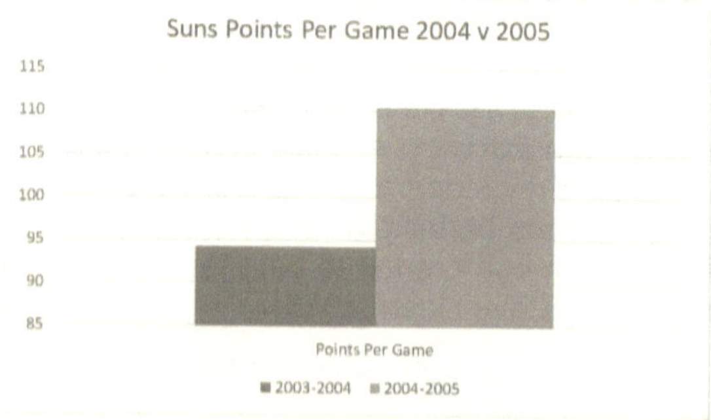

While the impact of the maturation of Amar'e Stoudemire, the addition of sixth man Quentin Richardson, and a full offseason for Coach Mike D'Antoni should not be discounted, but the next season revealed just how valuable Nash was to the team — they lost Amar'e to injury and only had eight fewer wins. (Wikipedia, n.d.).

"Steve is not just a great player. He's one of
the few players who I believe have ever played who
makes everyone better around him."
– Suns Chairman, Jerry Colangelo (Associated Press,
2006)

How did Steve make the difference? Scoring, but most especially **his passing**. With 11.5 assists per game, he set up shots for his teammates at a rate of almost a dozen per game. Simply put, Steve made everyone around him better. Suns Chairman, Jerry Colangelo best summed it up when he said "Steve is not just a great player. He's one of the few players who I believe have ever played who makes everyone better around him" (Associated Press, 2006).

In 2016 Microsoft MVPs gave 22,000 presentations,
answered 70,000 questions, made 140,000 open source
contributions, sent 800,000 tweets, and posted 16 million
additional social media comments.

In a similar fashion, **Microsoft Most Valuable Professionals (MVPs)** also make everyone else around them better. In 2016, 4000+ Microsoft MVPs gave over 22,000 presentations, answered 70,000 questions in forums, made 140,000 contributions to open source software through Github, wrote 800,000 tweets, posted 16 million additional social media comments, and published at least a dozen books (Tuffaha, 2017). Most of these activities were unpaid.

Why give away Knowledge?

Mark Minasi, one of the more prolific Microsoft MVPs (author of over 30 books, 300 magazine articles, and countless blog posts), likes to describe an old meme that sadly rings true of much of the tech world. Imagine two techies encountering each other for the first time, slinging acronyms at each other until "one bares his throat in submission." In a world where Knowledge is Power and Job Security, WHY would Mark and other Microsoft MVPs give away such valuable Knowledge?

This is the cumulative drive of the Microsoft Most Valuable Professionals -- to encourage others and to help everyone around them be better. Ok, sometimes we (the Microsoft MVPs) want to show off or can't stand the fact that people are relying on incorrect information, but mostly we do it for the intrinsic rewards that come from serving.

In a world where Scoring = Fame and Glory, WHY pass the ball?

Steve Nash recognized that he could help his team win more games by combining his talents for scoring and passing. He put the team above himself and was rewarded with back-to-back MVP awards.

Selfless Play

"Zobrist came to Wrigley Field without an ego. He played primarily at second base but also spent time in left field and right field. Always without complaint. Always with the greater goal in mind." – (AP, 2016)

Another great example of selfless play comes from Ben Zobrist. In 2016, the Chicago Cubs were seeking to end their 108-year drought – the last time they won the World Series had been in 1908. After making it to the 2015 National League Championship series (non-baseball fans: think "semi-finals") and losing, fans were frenzied after having been teased. Determined not to disappoint them,

Theo Epstein (Cubs President of Baseball Operations) made several bold changes to the team, among them adding Ben Zobrist to the roster. Ben had just hit a record EIGHT doubles in the playoffs to help the Kansas City Royals become World Series Champions. Theo described Ben as "one of the more valuable players in the game for a long time." An Associated Press article on Ben praised him, saying, "Zobrist came to Wrigley Field without an ego. He played primarily at second base but also spent time in left field and right field. Always without complaint. Always with the greater goal in mind" (AP, 2016).

In my interview with Ben, he explained how he integrated into his teams. "When I got to the major leagues, I found my way, I found things that worked for me that help me be valuable to the teams I was on… I play a lot of different positions, so whatever the team needs me to do I have to be willing and able to do those things."

The move paid off for Theo Epstein (and millions of Cub fans). During the 2016 World Series, Ben batted .357. Counting his walks, he got on base almost 42% of the times he stepped up to the plate. In the tenth inning of Game 7 (the series was tied at three wins each, with the score tied at 6-6) he focused on getting contact with the ball rather than dreaming of the glory of hitting a World Series-winning homerun. With two strikes against him, Ben fouled off a pitch, then hit a double that enabled teammate Albert Almora Jr. to score the go-ahead run (AP, 2016).

One could say that Ben won the MVP award by being flexible and versatile. At the very least, his versatility put him in a position to win the MVP award.

Steve Young (Football)

 On August 5, 1994, I eagerly attended an NFL preseason game, to see quarterback Steve Young and the San Francisco 49ers visit the Arizona Cardinals and begin their journey to winning Super Bowl XXIX (and Steve's journey towards winning his second NFL MVP). Naturally, they lost that game 7 to 17, and Steve Young played only sparingly.

That season, however, Young set records, having the best season as an NFL passer EVER until Peyton Manning's 2004 season a decade later. He started all 16 regular season games, threw 70.3% of his passes for completions, and threw for 35 touchdowns and only 10 interceptions. He led his team to a league best 13-3 record. In the first two playoff victories Steve Young turned in good but modest performances. In Game 1, he completed 16 of 22 passes for 143 yards (one for a touchdown) and running for an additional touchdown (Pro Football Reference, n.d.). In Game 2, he completed 13 of 29 passes for 155 yards and two touchdowns, running for an additional touchdown (Pro Football Reference, n.d.).

> "Steve threw 36 passes (24 for completions) for a total of 325 yards and a Super Bowl record SIX touchdowns!"

However, when the Super Bowl rolled around, Steve and his offensive coordinator Mike Shanahan really uncorked it. Steve threw 36 passes (24 for completions) for a total of 325 yards and a Super Bowl record SIX touchdowns! Wow! As if that were not impressive enough, Steve also did not throw a single interception during the playoffs (Pro Football Reference, n.d.)

Dale "The Murph" Murphy (Baseball)

On June 3, 1988, my grandparents took my baseball-crazed younger brother and me to San Diego's Jack Murphy Stadium to see Dale Murphy (our favorite player) and the Atlanta Braves face our home town San Diego Padres, led by Tony Gwynn and Gary Templeton (who also happened to be our neighbors; in fact, our bus stop was in front of Gwynn's house). We arrived plenty early to take in batting practice and sat only a few rows behind the visiting team dugout along the first base line. My brother brought a baseball in hopes of getting an autograph. After collecting signatures from any Brave he could get, he eventually got Dale Murphy to sign his baseball. In June of 1988 Dale Murphy was in a slump. He came into that game hitting .222 with only five home runs. In contrast, by June 3rd of the previous year he had already hit 14 home runs and was batting .317. That day he had two hits, both for home runs, and led the Braves to victory.

Dale, who played most of his career for the Atlanta Braves, hit more home runs and had more Runs Batted In (RBIs) than any other player in Major League Baseball over the ten-year period of 1981-1990, winning the National League MVP in 1982 and 1983. In 1982 he hit 36 home runs (2nd in the league), batted .280, and led the league with 109 RBIs. In his second consecutive National League MVP year, he again hit 36 home runs, batted .302 (a huge improvement), and led the league with 121 RBIs. He also stole 30 bases, pulling off a rare season in which someone steals 30 bases and hits 30 home runs, joining the so-called "30/30 Club." He also received the Golden Glove award several times for his excellent defense.

Mark Minasi

Virginia Beach, VA, USA

MVP 2003 – 2018

Category: Enterprise Mobility

Mark earned three degrees in math and economics and early on began using computers to model the latter. A self-described B- Coder, B+ economist, and A+ presenter, Mark was invited in 1983 to replace a speaker who went to see the Washington Redskins win the Super Bowl in Tampa. After a fascinating three-hour talk on computer graphics (at that time not much more than stick figures), he was told, "You're pretty good at [speaking and training]. Do you do this for a living?" His reply ("No, but I could.") was a pivotal moment in his career.

Mark is one of the most prolific and famous of the MVPs, having written at least 30 books and 300 articles in Windows IT Pro Magazine and others, as well as countless blog articles. Mark has also been in great demand speaking at conferences, even delivering the keynote addresses.

One of the driving forces behind Mark's passion to share his knowledge is an innate desire to keep people from "stumbling in the dark" while learning the intricate secrets of Windows.

Mark loves to teach and present. He shared with me his big secret: "I get more from them then they do from me." When someone asks him a great question, he says to himself, "Now, why didn't I think of that?"

Mark uses great analogies and metaphors in his teaching. During our interview, he related how computers have been his 'seven league boots' that have enabled him to fulfill his childhood dreams of writing a bestselling book and having a column in a magazine.

> "'I get more from [my students] then they do from me.'
> When someone asks him a great question, he says to himself,
> 'Now, why didn't I think of that?'"

https://twitter.com/mminasi
https://www.linkedin.com/in/mark-minasi-4a957b14/
http://www.minasi.com/mb2.htm
David's Book Reviews, Notes and Videos on DavidPLundell.com

Ben Zobrist (Baseball)

"You don't really think of it as extraordinary; you're just taking care of your business. You are trying to help others around you be the best version of themselves. "
– Ben Zobrist, 2016 World Series MVP

As noted earlier, Ben earned MVP honors in the 2016 World Series. He also earned the Northwoods League (college) MVP Award in 2003 while leading his team to the league championship (Conley, 2016). In 2009 Ben had his best year statistically. His combined offensive and defensive efforts had FanGraphs valuing him at the very top of the major league in Wins Above Replacement (WAR – a somewhat controversial measure that was developed to try and measure the true comprehensive value of a player). In 2009 Ben was given a WAR value of 8.6. This was better than Albert Pujols, the man who won the 2009 NL MVP (8.4 WAR in 2009) and Joe Mauer, the 2009 AL MVP winner (7.6 WAR) (FanGraphs, 2009). In other words, FanGraphs was saying that Ben should have been the AL MVP that year, if everyone really understood a baseball player's true value. Regardless, Ben had a great year with 27 home runs, a .297 batting average, and 91 RBIs. He finished 8th in the MVP voting and was an All-Star (Baseball Reference, n.d.).

During our interview Ben remarked that, "You don't really think of it as extraordinary; you're just taking care of your business." What he said next truly fits in with what I believe an MVP is: "You are trying to help others around you be the best version of themselves. If you care about the team, you care about winning, … you end up doing things that … you didn't know were possible at the time."

If you care about the team, you care about winning...
you end up doing things that personally
you didn't know were possible at the time."

Sid "the Kid" Crosby (Hockey)

In 2007 the Pittsburgh Penguins' Sid "the Kid" Crosby, from Halifax, Canada, scored 36 goals, and had 84 passes that resulted in goals (assists), leading the league with 120 points. He won the Hart Memorial Trophy (the NHL MVP). In 2014 he again led the league with 104 points (36 goals and 68 assists), once more winning the Hart Memorial Trophy. Sid's masterful passing, scoring, and leadership have led his Penguins to three Stanley Cups (NHL championships) in 2009, 2016, and 2017, and he was honored with a Conn Smythe Trophy (NHL's playoffs MVP award).

Steve Nash (Basketball)

On January 2, 2012, I eagerly used my Phoenix Suns Season Ticket Package to take my youngest son to the game to see Steve Nash play. In the first quarter, with the Suns down by six points (18-12) and in danger of losing their hold on the game, Steve made a nice jumper from the elbow to close the gap. In the 3rd quarter, with the score tied at 55-55, Nash stole a crosswise pass and made a fast break "alley-oop" pass to Grant Hill, who made a nice shot to put the Suns up by two points. If you'd like to see those highlights for yourself, visit https://www.youtube.com/watch?v=ArmMagXvAK4. Steve finished with 21 points and served up nine assists to lead the Suns to victory over the Golden State Warriors. It was a fantastic performance, although I would have loved to have seen his game on January 8 when he handed out 17 assists and only scored ten points.

In Steve Nash's 18-year NBA career, and in addition to twice being the league MVP, he was an All-Star eight times, selected to the All-NBA team seven times, led the league in assists per game five times, and led the league in total assists six times. He ended his career with 10,335 assists (behind only John Stockton and Jason Kidd) and 17,387 points scored. He also holds the NBA career free throw percentage record, hitting 90.42% of his career free throws (Basketball Reference, n.d.).

MVP Awards - Envy

In sports, everybody knows what an MVP is, and nearly everyone wants to be the MVP. Some want it for the glory, while some want it as a recognition of their valued contributions to their team. As I kid I was no different, but I never won the MVP in any physical team sport I played recreationally or at the high school level. I never led any league in goals, touchdowns, points, or assists. I never went on to play college sports or professional sports, let alone become a top professional athlete and win MVP awards like Steve Nash in basketball, Dale Murphy in baseball, Sid "The Kid" Crosby in hockey, or Steve Young in football. In 1993, the only college football team that wanted my athletic prowess was a Division III team that had gone winless the year before and was more renowned for their academics than athletics.

However, in my academic and professional life I can say I have done much better than I did athletically. Starting in 2007, and each year for the next 11 years since then, Microsoft has awarded me the Microsoft Most Valuable Professional (MVP) Award for my contributions to Microsoft's community of Identity Management professionals.

Suddenly I was part of an elite group. In 2007 only seven people in the world were accorded MVP status for Microsoft's Identity Management product. Almost overnight, people started paying more attention to things I wrote and said.

In 2010 I wrote the first ever book about Microsoft's Identity Management product. I went to Germany to speak at "The Experts Conference" Europe (TEC Europe as it was known), and at the welcome reception people spontaneously lined up to speak with me and get my autograph in their copies of my book. Even seven years later, at the Consumer Identity World 2017 conference in Seattle, a happy fan of my book (now a guru in his own right) thanked me and wanted my autograph. Every time it was – and continues to be – a bit surreal.

> In 2007 only seven people in the world were accorded MVP status for Microsoft's Identity Management Product.

So, within a narrow set of interested people (Microsoft Identity Management nerds/geeks – I am one), I became internationally famous.

As nice as the recognition has been for my ego, the real rewards have been the intrinsic ones – knowing that I was able to help people at work and in the community to be better.

What is a Tech MVP?

This is a term that I created to describe Microsoft MVPs in a more general way and to be able to include other technology professionals who do what Microsoft MVPs do.

What is the Microsoft MVP?

This is the highest award that Microsoft gives out to non-employees. It is an award, not a certification. The award is given to recognize an individual's contributions to the technical community (writing blogs, answering questions on forums, writing wikis, speaking at conferences and user groups, writing books and magazine articles). Individuals from organizations large and small have received it. Even non-IT people who are passionate about a specific tech have received it. There is no clearly delineated path to "earn" the award.

Microsoft pointed out that "of the more than 100 million social and technical community members worldwide, each year only about 3,800 are recognized as MVPs" (Becoming an MVP, 2015). For most of us, our passion for how to use a specific product or set of technologies led us to develop technical expertise and resulted in us trying to tell the world about something cool we found.

"Of the more than 100 million social
and technical community members
worldwide, each year only about
3,800 are recognized as MVPs."
– (Becoming an MVP, 2015)

As MVPs, Microsoft doesn't tell us what to say, but they do often give us sneak previews or even solicit our input before making design decisions, recognizing that we are often thought leaders in our communities.

MVP 25th Anniversary

The MVP program started in 1993, recognizing the efforts of people answering questions on CompuServe forums, well before the Internet became so popular.

In early 2018, to commemorate the 25th anniversary of the Microsoft MVP program, the MVP Award program set a goal to encourage MVPs in each of the four geographical regions to make 25 significant contributions (pull requests) to the allReady project – an open source software project to support emergency awareness/preparedness campaigns led by Microsoft MVP James Chambers.

How do you become a Microsoft MVP?

You must be nominated, and your contributions must be evaluated, as MVPs are expected to make significant contributions to their technical community. In life people often say, "It's not *what* you know, but *who* you know." I tend to think that with the Microsoft MVP program, the quote should be, "It's *what* you know, and *who* sees you sharing it."

"It's what you know and who sees you sharing it."

However, you need to be nominated by an active MVP or a Microsoft employee. You used to be able to nominate yourself. "Potential MVPs are nominated by other technical community members, current and former MVPs, and Microsoft personnel who have noted their community leadership" (Becoming an MVP, 2015). Also, just being nominated doesn't mean you will receive the award, as your contributions will be evaluated to see if you measure up to the level of MVP. Every year the contributions of existing MVPs are evaluated, and to receive the award again you must continue to make contributions.

"Potential MVPs are nominated by other technical community members, current and former MVPs, and Microsoft personnel who have noted their community leadership."
— (Becoming an MVP, 2015)

What kinds of contributions do Microsoft MVPs make?

- Answering questions in online forums like:
  - answers.com
  - social.msdn.microsoft.com/forums
  - social.technet.microsoft.com/forums
- Building open source solutions
  - Coding
  - Testing
  - Documenting
- Enhancing Microsoft documentation
- Leading (and speaking to) user groups
- Organizing or presenting at conferences
- Writing articles
- Blog posts
- Social media posts
- Writing books
- Feedback to the Microsoft Product groups

Rob Prouse

Hamilton, ON, Canada

MVP 2017 – Present

Category: Visual Studio and

Development Technologies

My interview with Rob at the MVP summit in November of 2016 was unique, as he was not an MVP, nor had he been. Rob had been nominated towards the beginning of the year, but his paperwork was mislaid. However, Microsoft invited him to the summit anyhow. Rob knew little about the MVP program before being nominated, but is happy to be "recognized for [his] open source work." Rob has been a dot net (.NET) developer since 1.0, and is much heartened by Microsoft's shift in policy to start supporting Open Source libraries for .NET. Rob has put in a great deal of time leading the effort on NUnit (the most popular unit testing framework – currently at 13 million downloads).

Rob leads the local users group, having found that one of the best ways to learn is to teach. Additionally, he attends conferences and reads curated blog lists.

Originally, Rob served in the Canadian Armed Forces for ten years. After his service, he needed a new career and decided to simply walk unannounced into a game development company. He convinced them to take a chance on him with the offer to "pay me nothing and give me six months," which led to a raise – to a decent, actual wage, that is. Rob also realized that one of the core skills of being a developer is communication; as he is very introverted, he worked hard to be able to talk to people and understand their business requirements and business problems.

"Recognized for [his] open source work, ... NUnit, ...
currently at 13 million downloads"

https://mvp.microsoft.com/en-us/PublicProfile/5002349
https://twitter.com/rprouse
https://www.linkedin.com/in/robprouse/
Rob: David's notes and videos on DavidPLundell.com

How do we know when we do excellent work?

Professional sports have great statistics we can use to measure how well athletes do, but how do we know when we and others are doing excellent work?

 When a project of yours has been downloaded 13 million times, it is highly probably your work is excellent (and has a broad market). Rob Prouse, a recently awarded Microsoft MVP and a ten-year veteran of the Canadian Armed Forces, has for years led the effort to develop NUnit, an open source (meaning it is free) testing framework that makes software developers much more effective at making bug-free software.

Kathy Jacobs, a previous Outlook and later OneNote MVP and author, was in such demand that she delivered 30 presentations in 21 days to different user groups around the Phoenix Area. She accomplished this feat not once but on three separate occasions.

Hal Hostetler, Microsoft MVP since 1996, said that "The biggest gratification from that has always been the thank you notes that I get in the email. I've got a collection of thank you notes from everybody from garbage collectors to heads of state."

> "I've got a collection of thank you notes from everybody
> from **garbage collectors** to **heads of state**."
> – Hal Hostetler, Microsoft MVP since 1996

Writing 12 books and getting over 100,000 views for several technical videos provides great evidence of the superlative work of Sheffield UK based Mike Halsey, a Microsoft MVP since 2011.

For Mark Minasi, having a book that *only* sold 30,000 copies was a disappointment. His more than 40 books tended to target a broader audience (Microsoft Windows) than many MVP's are targeting (for example, Microsoft Identity Manager, where selling almost 2,000 copies is great!).

Michael Washington has been an MVP since 2007, and has written nine books. Michael also does extensive blogging, and even created forums as a place to host questions for specific technologies before Microsoft created their own official forums.

In 2009, then-future MVP Andy Milford got a pretty good indicator of the value of his work when he sold his software company to IpSwitch. He became a serial entrepreneur upon founding his second company. When speaking at an industry event, a program manager from Microsoft praised his presentation and in effect nominated him to be an MVP.

Rob Richardson (twitter handle RobRich), like Rob Prouse, spends a lot of free time contributing to open source software. Rob's favorite project is called Gulp JS, where he is one of 22 contributors according to GitHub. Gulp JS helps programmers streamline their dev workflow. The project has over 162,000 installs and claims to have help saved an infinite number of seconds.

In the cases of Dale Murphy, Steve Nash, Ben Zobrist, Sidney Crosby, and Steve Young, their high-level performances resulted in being paid millions of dollars, acclaim in the press, and many awards (including their MVP awards). Most of the Microsoft MVPs have been similarly rewarded, albeit on a smaller scale, with pay in the tens and hundreds of thousands of dollars, acclaim on user forums, and the MVP Award from Microsoft.

We do get feedback when we answer questions on forums, because the original poster has the chance to mark it as the answer and others can mark it as helpful. We can also see how many people read our blog posts, how many people buy our books, how many people watch our videos, and how many people see us speak. However, most of the Microsoft MVPs with whom I spoke, while aware of the number of touches, truly measure the worth of their contributions in the emotions – how it made them feel when someone said, "Thanks! That was a big help! That saved my bacon!"

What about things that aren't so easily measured or that take years before we get to hear a "thank-you?"

Those of you who are parents should easily relate to this question. My approach to this is to first recognize that not everything with my family or my community efforts (coaching football, serving as a Cub and Boy Scout leader) are under my control. Kids have an increasing ability to choose for themselves what they will do. At best we may have influence over the outcome, but certainly not control. However, by focusing on the things we DO control, we can increase our influence.

For example, my co-coach (Jeff Rozdilsky) and I may want our flag football team to have a championship season, but that is outside of our control (and admittedly not even our focus). Don't get me wrong, we want the kids to win, but even more than that we want them to be successful. Jeff says, "Winning is scoring more points than the other team. Success is when we do our best and improve." In my coaching experience, I have been part of teams that ended the season in each of the top three places. I have also been part of teams that were far from one of the top three.

Jeff and I can't control if kids show up for practice, but we can influence their decision to attend by making practice exciting, reminding the kids and the parents, and showing up on time and prepared.

Parenting is similar. My wife and I can't force our children to get top grades, but we can set expectations, make ourselves available to help, eliminate distractors, attend parent teacher conferences, and review their progress.

In both cases, if we aren't seeing the results we hope for, we go back to things we can control and make changes there.

For instance, three of my kids have dyslexia, which is a significant challenge to their academic success. No matter how motivated they were, they still struggled with reading (and especially with spelling). We learned what we could about dyslexia, we hired a very experienced private tutor, and when our school district offered effective programs to help dyslexics we enrolled our kids into those programs.

Like Stephen Covey encourages us in his famous 7 habits book, we should "Be Proactive" and focus on the things we CAN control.

Personal Value – Market Gravity

In Alan Weiss's book Million Dollar Consulting, he espouses an idea that I believe captures the personal value of playing extremely well, or being an MVP. He calls it "market gravity." As you develop market gravity, people come to you. The value in this is obvious. In the sports world, the athlete who becomes an MVP can command a very high salary. For a consultant, your cost of sales is much lower when people come to you. As a staff consultant, your value to a consulting firm increases if you bring business to them as people seek you out. For the MVP not involved in consulting, she or he can draw more talented engineers into the company and onto their team as they build amazing things together.

What's even better than being a sports MVP or a Microsoft MVP? Being an MVP In Life!

We can't all be pro sports MVPs like Steve Nash, Dale Murphy, Steve Young, or Sid the Kid Crosby. We can't all be Microsoft MVPs. But we can each be an MVP in Life. We can each work to make others around us better at home, at work, and in the community, strengthening our families, making work more fulfilling, and serving in our various communities. In short, by each of us striving to be an MVP in Life, we are also working towards building a better world.

How do you become an MVP In Life?

The first thing you must realize is that there is no magic secret or special system that will make everything get done and make your dreams come true. What there is, however, is a way to live (or a system) that makes all the struggle worthwhile, that inspires you, and that helps you to be happy along the way and not just at the mythical end.

How does this help me become a Microsoft MVP?

One thing that Microsoft MVPs are known for is being experts. In order to be considered for the award, you must have expertise in one or more technologies. As you read about me (and other Microsoft MVPs), our examples will hopefully lead the way. Additionally, I will include exercises to help you find your own path.

Action Plan: How do you want to measure yourself?

When thinking about how to measure yourself it is important that you come at it from the perspective expressed by Simon Sinek in his now famous book <u>Start With Why</u>, so that your measurements reflect back to your raison d'etre, your "reason for getting out of bed each morning."

As I mentioned before, in sports there are all kinds of statistics to measure the performance of each athlete. However, within the last 10-30 years, each of the major sports have developed new metrics: in baseball, sabermetrics gave us the Wins Above Replacement (WAR); in basketball, we have the Player Efficiency Rating (PER) and the Plus/Minus (which they brought over from Hockey); and in football, they recently added a QBR, or total quarterback rating, to measure everything a quarterback does and not just focusing on his passing. Even in these sports, where certain metrics were considered hallowed and *the* definitive way to measure success, things have been redefined.

So, how do you want to measure yourself? Feel free to write your answer here or in your own notebook or journal, but really take some time to think about your answers. If you are looking for a good place to start, or would like a supplementary resource on this topic, I strongly encourage you to check out the 2012 book <u>How Will *You* Measure Your Life</u> by Clayton M Christensen, James Allworth, and Karen Dillon.

- *How do you want to measure yourself at work?*

- *How do you want to measure yourself in the community?*

- *How do you want to measure yourself at home?*

- *What can you do to address those items that are difficult to measure?*

What's next?

My goal is to tell the stories of many different MVP's (Microsoft MVPs and a few sports MVPs) so as to inspire you, the readers, in your efforts to make others around you better, because that is what it truly means to be an MVP -- Most Valuable Player -- Most Valuable Professional -- Most Valuable Person -- at home, at work, and in the community. I will also include brainstorming and planning activities, all to help you answer these three key Questions:

<u>Part II How do they perform so well?</u>

- <u>Chapter 2: Practice Constantly (Continuous Self-Improvement)</u>

- <u>Chapter 3: Listen to the Coach</u>

- <u>Chapter 4: Work through injuries and challenges</u>

<u>Part III How do MVPs help everyone else around them be better?</u>

- <u>Chapter 5: Passing the Ball</u>

- <u>Chapter 6: Praise your teammates</u>

- <u>Chapter 7: Care about the game and others</u>

<u>Part IV How can I be an MVP in Life?</u>

- <u>Chapter 8: Be the MVP</u>

David P Lundell

Part II How do they perform so well?

Steve Young led the league four times in touchdown passes and six times in passer rating, Dale Murphy led the league in Home runs twice, RBI's twice, Runs once, Slugging Percentage twice, On Base Plus Slugging once, and walks once. Sidney Crosby led the league in Points Per Game in 5 amazing seasons. Similarly, Steve Nash also led his league 5 times in Assists per Game.

So, with their outstanding individual performances, MVP's are amazing, but how do they become that way?

- <u>Chapter 2: Practice Constantly (Continuous Self-Improvement)</u>
- <u>Chapter 3: Listen to the Coach (Be Teachable)</u>
- <u>Chapter 4: Work through injuries and challenges (Perseverance)</u>

David P Lundell

Chapter 2: Practice Constantly (Continuous Self-Improvement)

Benched (Steve Nash)

Gretchen (Opferkew) Mann

Expanding your skills through helping others

Sid "the Kid" Crosby Starts Practice at 2

Microsoft MVPs

Work Harder and Longer (Ben Zobrist)

Dale Murphy and Steve Young

Jessica Moss

The Personal Value of Continuous Improvement

Action Plan: Am I practicing enough?

Benched (Steve Nash)

Once he reached the highest level of basketball with the Phoenix Suns, Steve Nash had to cope with playing second string to an All-Star point guard, Kevin Johnson. Even worse, during that first season, his team traded for the league's top point guard, Jason Kidd. If I had been in his shoes, that wouldn't really have made me feel like my team thought I was the point guard of the future.

How did Nash react?

"My main concern was how I'm going to make myself better, so I can be successful – regardless of who's here." – Steve Nash (as a rookie)

Rather than get angry or fall into despair, Steve Nash took a very healthy approach. "My main concern was how I'm going to make myself better, so I can be successful -- regardless of who's here." He also understood that the coach would make the best decisions for the team, after all, and he "probably didn't deserve a lot of minutes" since they "had two All-star point guards" (Geracie, 1998).

Sitting out, but improving your game

This work ethic was evident all the way back in Nash's high school days. After Steve's parents, worried about his slipping academics, transferred him to a new high school, he had to sit out a whole season. "He made up for not being on the team by practicing every waking hour." Even on his way to school, "He would dribble a ball… using first the right hand, then the left hand." After school he took hundreds of free throws. Hmm, taking hundreds of free throw shots per day might have something to do with why Steve holds the NBA record for career free throw shooting percentage. "Not being able to play might actually have made him a better player because he focused so hard on practicing" (Bailey, 2007).

> Taking hundreds of free throw shots per day might have something to do with why Steve holds the NBA record for career free throw shooting percentage

Once Nash was at Santa Clara University, he discovered he needed to work even harder when John Woolery, starting point guard, "regularly made him look bad in practice" (Bailey, 2007). Nash's response as described by Woolery is quite exemplary: "Some guys [after looking so bad] would shy away from the ball. But he'd want to do it again and again…until he could get it right." Authors Dave Feschuk and Michael Grange summarized Woolery's comments, saying, "Nash, like a kid trying to master a video game, would hit some kind of mental reset button and began the battle afresh" (Feschuk, 2014).

In his interview with Charles Foran, Steve revealed that he truly understood that "Natural talent is only potential." He explained that to realize your potential "You have to combine it with other things-- confidence, hard work, even daring." Nash certainly applied his own advice, explaining, "I try to come early every day to work. I put in a lot of time" (Foran, 2005).

Gretchen (Opferkew) Mann

Minneapolis, MN, USA

MVP 2012-2017

Category: Business Solutions (Dynamics CRM)

Before being nominated to be an MVP, Gretchen participated in many online Microsoft Dynamics CRM forums. She also served on the board of an online international CRM users' group. As a programming committee member, she always tried to give others a chance to shine. She glowingly recounted the joy when many people she encouraged to speak came back to her later, exclaiming, "I used to see you speak and now I am speaking!"

She has seen great rewards from speaking in the Dynamics Academics Alliance, where she has had a chance to help and influence college students.

Gretchen calls her career in the technology industry her "accidental career." She first worked for a non-profit, and once lived in Africa for a year. After ten years and seven schools, she sought a degree to manage non-profits. She worked in the technology field while seeking her degree, and upon graduation she was already managing a team of consultants.

She wanted to make the world a better place and now uses technology to do just that. Gretchen also spends time mentoring her teammates, focusing on the one-one one career path discussions and helping people play to their strengths.

When people ask Gretchen how to become an MVP, she encourages them to be their best authentic self, rather than an imitation of someone else. For example, since Gretchen is more reflective as opposed to outspoken, she writes contemplative articles rather than sitting on panels where she needs to speak off the cuff.

> "When people ask Gretchen how to become an MVP,
> she encourages them to be their best authentic self,
> rather than an imitation of someone else"

https://twitter.com/CRMGretchen

https://www.linkedin.com/in/crmgretchen/

https://mvp.microsoft.com/en-us/PublicProfile/5000178

Gretchen: David's notes and videos on DavidPLundell.com

Expanding your skills through helping others

In 2004-2006 I became aware of the need for answers on forums. At that time, I was focused on SQL Server, Microsoft's enterprise database platform that many companies did (and do) use to run their businesses. I was teaching a lot of SQL Server classes, and so I started answering questions on a few forums. I became aware of the MVP program from Microsoft and I wanted to be a SQL Server (Data Platform) MVP. However, the field was very competitive. It seemed as though people were answering on the Microsoft SQL forums within 30 seconds of a question being asked. So, I found other forums where people's questions were going unanswered, and I started helping them. In a few months, when students and other contacts searched my name on the web, that became the most prevalent of the search results, which gave me instant credibility with my students. After a while I stopped worrying about the MVP status and just focused on improving myself in ways that would make me more valuable to my clients, primarily teaching and consulting. When I wasn't busy teaching or consulting, I answered forum questions. It became an addiction and many people were impressed with my knowledge and grateful for the help.

In 2006 I encountered the field of Identity Management (IdM). As I learned about Microsoft's product in this field, I realized that I could utilize my skills with databases, directories, and programming to automate giving people user accounts and taking them away when they left! Back when I had been in the IT department at a Fortune 500 home builder, I had longed for such a solution. Soon, I fell in love with Identity Management (although I still love my wife more).

> The more I helped others,
> the more I was viewed as an expert, and
> the greater my opportunities to teach and consult!

As I started learning, I also began answering questions right away, using my varied background with databases, directories, and programming to come up with new solutions. As I continued consulting and training, I did more and more Identity Management. During downtimes I was absolutely hooked – I answered question after question. Each time I encountered something new and not readily answerable from the documentation, I would recreate the scenario in the lab and then provide answers, sometimes spending 2-3 hours on each individual question.

As I answered the questions, my knowledge grew in leaps and bounds, primarily because I had solved problems that I wouldn't have even encountered otherwise. Helping others with their questions provided me constant practice across a broad range of situations. The more I helped others, the more I was viewed as an expert, and the greater my opportunities to teach and consult!

Very soon I was viewed as an expert in the field. In rapid succession, I began taking advantage of the opportunity to start speaking at conferences, and I became a Microsoft MVP.

Sid "the Kid" Crosby Starts Practice at 2

That is at AGE TWO, not 2 AM, that Sidney Crosby began practicing hockey. At that age, Sid "the Kid" Crosby began launching pucks against the clothes dryer in his family basement and at age three he learned to ice skate (Sidney Crosby, n.d.). I wonder how many family dryers were sacrificed to Sid's practice?

Microsoft MVPs

Right Attitude and Challenging work

For Microsoft MVP Pablo Di Loreto, his Argentinian attitude is the key to staying on the cutting edge. "Don't believe you know everything, always orient to the fountain of all knowledge, always analyze, [and finally] always ask if you don't understand." Remaining teachable and always trying to improve are two universal keys to success.

Virtuous Cycle

Like me, Jessica Moss sees a virtuous cycle in "working on the forums." Simply put, by helping others we learn and increase our own expertise. She loves how "looking at problems from different people has a way" of giving a fresh perspective and helps you to "think of things in a different way." Jessica loves to stretch and grow as she encounters questions outside her area of expertise (Business Intelligence and SQL Server), finding great excitement in "learning more about … coding, SharePoint and Identity Management." We agreed that what people do in other areas might even be applicable to your own area. You could say that Jessica's motto is "Oh! What does that mean? Let me find out!"

> "Looking at problems from different
> people [helps me to] think of
> doing things in a different way."
> – Jessica Moss, Microsoft MVP

Surfing ahead of the trends

For Chicago-based author and Microsoft MVP Joe Kaplan, most of his proscribed activities for staying sharp flow through the work he does. His role, as an IT staff guy, in contrast to a consultant, is to design the fresh and new things to stay ahead of the trends (and the bad guys) to safely provide employees, contractors, and partners access to his employer's resources. Joe does confess that since he focuses on his organization's specific problems, he doesn't get the breadth of technical experience that others might, but he certainly gets the depth. For those interested in the debate about on premise vs. the cloud, Joe's forecast is that on-premise directories (like Active Directory) will be around for quite a while (and may never go away); nonetheless, he believes that federated identity and identity in the cloud is the way of the future.

Stretching oneself

Then a Microsoft Dynamics CRM (Business Solutions) MVP, now a Microsoft employee, Gretchen (Opferkew) Mann continuously seeks to improve herself. She is always seeking to learn new technology and new features, even when they are not associated with her day job. She is constantly reading articles, blogs, and books (especially during flights), and she follows other experts in the field on Twitter and LinkedIn. But watch out! She keeps her Twitter feed *very* focused. She cares about your technical content, not what you had for lunch or if you are upset at your airline. Those that start adding politics or religion into the conversations get dropped quickly, because Gretchen decides who to follow – and who to *continue* following – for their technical content, and she is happy getting all of the other content elsewhere. She is an invaluable resource for many others.

Gretchen is acutely aware that being an expert in one discipline doesn't automatically make a person an expert in other areas. Sensing a need to improve her public speaking abilities, she joined and actively participates in Toastmasters.

Constant Service

Rob Prouse, our aforementioned Canadian MVP who leads the NUnit delivery, hones his skills by learning, doing, and teaching. He follows several curated blog lists, attends conferences, works on NUnit for "several hours a day," and presents at user groups. Rob once quipped that the "best way to learn things is to teach them," and he certainly lives by that motto.

Those who can, do; those who can't, teach themselves how to do

Arizona based MVP Clint Wyckoff has a similar approach. "I force myself to go and learn -- pick a topic I know nothing about and blog about it. I have to research and become knowledgeable." Many other MVPs have similar attitudes.

Work Harder and Longer (Ben Zobrist)

Ben keeps his baseball skills honed with "every day practice" for hours a day. Ben also noticed that with baseball you are "performing every day, not just practicing." This is closer to how most of us in business operate – we are, as Ben said, "put to the test regularly." Therefore, we must be "prepared to do that skill when it really counts."

Ben's father recounts that "he was always willing to work harder and longer than any coach expected… He would sprint around the track when he was supposed to be jogging." Despite being a pitcher in college, Ben still wanted to be a shortstop. But, "the coaches wouldn't let him field ground balls during practice." So, Ben would take ground balls on his own time. Once, after a doubleheader, his Dad waited for him for an hour, "so [Ben] could take ground balls" (Zobrist, 2017).

> "He was always willing to work harder
> and longer than any coach expected."
> – Tom Zobrist about his son Ben, 2016 WS MVP

Dale Murphy and Steve Young

While some of the incredible stories about the practice habits and work ethics of Dale Murphy and Steve Young would enhance the lessons presented in this chapter, they are best told in the context of the next chapter, "Listen to the Coach," so we will save them for later.

Jessica Moss

Richmond, VA, USA

MVP 2008- 2018

Category: Data Platform

Jessica began her MVP journey in Tampa's SQL User Group Meeting, back when Microsoft SQL Server Business Intelligence was very new. Feedback from her first presentation "was the bug that bit [her]," and has kept her hooked ever since. She also spoke at the SQL Pass Summit in 2008 (I saw that talk – it was awesome). She continues to speak at SQL Teach, SQL Connections, and SQL Saturdays.

In addition to getting her name out there, Jessica loves giving people knowledge – especially when she can 'see' the light bulb above their heads power on and illuminate their minds. An early chance to shine came when Jessica was invited to co-present at SQL Teach and ended up presenting solo when her co-worker couldn't attend.

Jessica feels lucky about the challenges she has faced, although she admits some of those challenges were self-inflicted, noting that, "Most people have been welcoming and helpful." She hates writing but has co-authored or contributed to eight books. She "took four months off from work to write four chapters," learning that it got easier with time.

Jessica advocates answering forum questions as a means of self-improvement, emphasizing how looking at the problems of different people inspires thinking about things in a different way.

Ms. Moss also gives back in a variety of ways: volunteering at United Way, Meals on Wheels, painting school walls (not graffiti!), and her University of Virginia alumni group.

"Jessica advocates answering forum questions
as a means of self-improvement,
emphasizing how looking at the problems of different people
inspires thinking about things in a different way."

https://mvp.microsoft.com/en-us/PublicProfile/4021853
https://www.linkedin.com/in/mossjessica/
David's reviews of Jessica's books and other notes on DavidPLundell.com

The Personal Value of Continuous Improvement

In Malcolm Gladwell's well-known book, <u>Outliers: The Story of Success,</u> he discusses the 10,000-hour rule.

Citing the writings of neurologist Daniel Levitin, "ten thousand hours of practice is required to achieve the level of mastery associated with being a world class expert." Although in a Reddit Ask Me Anything session he clarified that "Practice isn't a SUFFICIENT condition for success… [the] point is simply that natural ability requires a huge investment of time in order to be made manifest" (Gladwell, 2015). Of course, it should also be noted that the practice must be "deliberate practice," with almost instant feedback so that you practice correctly and correct your mistakes quickly.

However, don't confuse the means with the long-term goal. Constant practice is merely one of the means to the end, which must always be Continuous Self-Improvement.

In a November 18, 2013 blog post discussing his book <u>How to Fail at Almost Everything and Still Win Big</u>, Scott Adams, the creator of Dilbert, wrote about the need to have systems, citing his own example of how his "blogging was a system… [to] practice… writing" and to do "R&D for writing." He expounded about the value of systems over narrow, limiting goals. Continuous self-improvement is an example of just such a system. In each system, we have overarching goals that we work towards, but not limiting goals. Had I been too focused on my goal of becoming a SQL MVP instead of developing a system of continuous self-improvement (aimed at making myself more valuable to clients), I might have missed the opportunity to make a difference in the world of Identity Management.

Many of the Microsoft MVP's absolutely love tinkering with technology. It is fun and exciting. Many also love the feeling of being able to help someone, and some questions on the forum stretch them and enhance their expertise.

- What can you do that will help others and grow your skills?

4 Passion, Ability and Demand

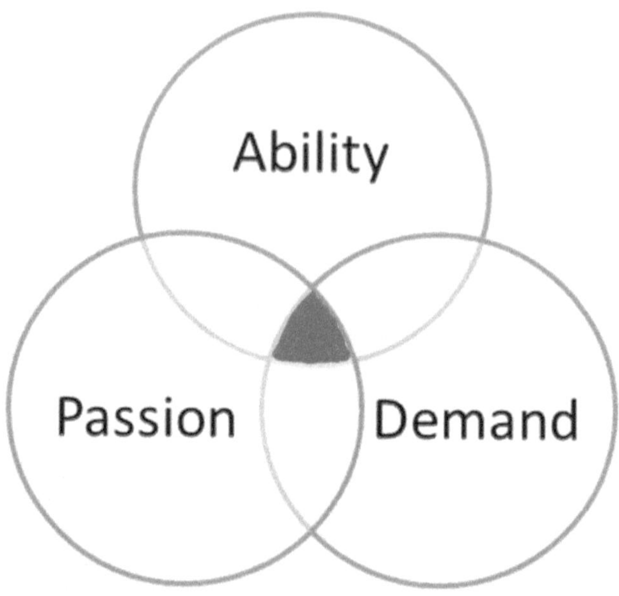

When I first started learning SQL Server (Microsoft's database server product), I was very passionate about it. I was constantly reading about it and trying out everything I read. I couldn't get enough. I began to have success with it, spending my time learning it, teaching it, managing it, and developing with it. However, after a few years I was no longer as passionate about SQL. It wasn't new, and I found something else I was passionate about: Identity Management. The key is to find something where your passion, ability and demand for that skill intersect.

Now that we have a common vocabulary and understanding, let me ask a few questions to provoke your thoughts and help you develop such a system for yourself.

Action Plan: Am I practicing enough?

Wrong question! Do not ask, "Am I practicing enough?" Instead, you should ask yourself (Once more take the time to write down your answers):

- What can I do to improve?
- How can I better channel my passions?
- How can I get addicted to doing something worthwhile that will also improve my skills?

Chapter 3: Listen to the Coach (Be Teachable)

MVP referred to the Instructional league

Nash and the Coaches Critiques

Clint Wyckoff

Really Humbling Experience (Ben Zobrist)

Seven Day Wonder, Humbled

Microsoft MVPs

Pablo Ariel Di Loreto

When is it best not to Listen to the Coach? (Steve Young)

Personal value of Listening to the Coach

Action Plan: Listening Better

MVP referred to the Instructional league

At the end of the 1982 Baseball season, the great Atlanta Braves Slugger Dale Murphy was voted the NL MVP, the Most Valuable Player in the National League (indicating that he was one of the two best players in all of Major League Baseball). Dale had hit 36 home runs (2nd in the league), batted in 109 runs (1st in the league), hit safely 28.1% of the time (.281 Batting Average), and yet his Manager (non-baseball fans, think Head Coach) Joe Torre suggested going to the instructional league -- where they send rookies and other struggling players. "As good as he was, I saw ways to improve his hitting" (Wulf, 1983).

What would you do?

Just imagine. That's like selling a million copies of your album and your coach says let's work on your scales or doing all the calculations that got the astronauts to the moon and back and then being invited to review your multiplication facts. Can you imagine any recent pro sports MVP possessing both the humility and the courage to play in their instructional/developmental league in the offseason?

What did Dale do?

"At first Murphy was surprised when Torre suggested he go to the Instructional League." After considering the suggestion, Dale realized he has some weaknesses; in 1982 Dale struck out 134 times vs 168 hits and 93 walks. Dale said he "thought it was a compliment that Joe wanted to take the time and go down there and work on a few things with [him]." He ultimately went, combining it with a planned trip to Disney World with his wife and two sons (Wulf, 1983).

The result?

The next year Dale got even better! In mid-season, Manager Joe Torre observed, "I think we are seeing the fruits of that work this year … he's become a much better hitter with two strikes on him" (Wulf, 1983). Dale struck out 24 fewer times (110), increased his batting average by 21 points (from .281 to .302), scored 18 more runs, and batted in 12 additional runs. Oh yeah, he also won the NL MVP Award. Again.

"He's become a much better hitter with two strikes on him." – Joe Torre, describing why Dale Murphy struck out 24 fewer times, hit 21 points higher, scored 18 more runs and batted in 12 additional runs.

The improvements stayed with him, as he returned batting averages of .290, .300, .265, and .295 over the next four years after that.

Nash and the Coaches Critiques

Nash and his various biographers credit his coaches with helping him realize his potential as a basketball player. "Ian [his HS coach] would even play Steve one-on-one, showing him the tricks of the trade, teaching him the fundamentals, and impressing on Steve how important a simple game plan was to success" (Bailey, 2007).

Coach Davey, who recruited Nash and then became the head coach at Santa Clara University, evaluated Nash as "the worst defensive player," and throughout his time gave Nash "plenty of frank assessments of [his] weak points" (Feschuk, 2014).

When Nash retired, he wrote a blog post and credited one his coaches, Mike D'Antoni, with "[changing] the game of basketball. There's not many people you can say that about. No wonder I had my best years playing for him." Mike didn't emphasize defense all that much so this could also be a case of playing to Nash's strengths, which is something else a good coach does. "His intelligence guided him to never over-coach, complicate or hide behind the game's traditions." He also praised, Alvin Gentry, indicating that he "coached the heck out of our teams… [and] found the elusive line between coach, friend and disciplinarian" (Nash, 2015).

Really Humbling Experience (Ben Zobrist)

Ben and three of his friends pool their collective 100 years' worth of baseball expertise in the "Show and Go Podcast" (https://theshowandgo.podbean.com/). In the latest episode (as of this writing) they discuss player-coach communication. They illustrate how listening with an open mind, and giving the coach the benefit of the doubt, can pay off for the player with solid ways to improve. They state that it is important to believe that the coach has "the best motive at heart" and to "assume that the coach is doing the best he can." If there is any ambiguity in the feedback, "ask [the coach] to clarify" what he or she meant.

After that insightful discussion, former major league and current minor league pitcher Tim Dillard shared a "really humbling experience." His manager brought in a "side arm specialist" to help him with his sinker pitch. At first Tim thought, "Hey, I used to be in the majors not that long ago," and wondered why he needed a specialist. The specialist asked him to show him his sinker, and he did. The specialist seemed unimpressed. "No, show me your sinker," he asked again. Two or three times that happened, and Tim felt like he was "about to rip the grass out." However, once Tim humbled himself "to be teachable [and] coachable" the specialist showed him a "different grip on the ball and it was amazing" (Dillard, 2018).

"Really humbling experience."
– Tim Dillard, on getting taught a new grip for his sinker,
despite being a former Big Leaguer.

Ben apparently benefited from coaching advice early on. "When Ben was in middle school, he set the high-jump record as a seventh grader, just because the coach asked him one time to try something different – a change of pace. He went to State in high jump both years [of middle school]" (Zobrist, 2017).

Ben's father credits Joe Maddon, who had been Ben's manager "for nine years in Tampa" and then again with the Cubs in Chicago, saying that "Joe's leadership is what made Ben a super utility player valuable beyond his abilities" (Zobrist, 2017).

Clint Wyckoff

Phoenix, AZ, USA

MVP 2016 – Present

Category: Cloud and

Datacenter Management

Clint loves giving back by sharing his knowledge. In fact, he has made quite a number of videos for Microsoft Channel 9, spoken at TechMentor and MVPDays virtual conference (which he also helped organize), and has contributed to a book.

In his role as an MVP, Clint has access to Microsoft program managers and enjoys helping them improve their products by sharing his knowledge via effective and directed feedback.

Clint stays on top of his game by reading blogs, talking with other people, and watching videos. His preferred activity is to pick a topic he knows nothing about and research it thoroughly until he feels knowledgeable enough to blog about it.

Clint heaps a lot of praise on Dave and Cristal Kawula, two Canadian MVPs who (among others) took him under their wings and "taught [him] how to write a proper blog post." They also gave him a chance to edit and contribute to the book they co-authored with several others on a Microsoft cloud product.

Clint is no stranger to life threatening challenges. When he was 28, he was diagnosed with cancer. He persevered, never quitting, never saying "die", and never taking "no" for an answer. Reflecting on this experience has helped him be a better parent and instill values in his kids, and he now helps coach his son's hockey team.

> "He persevered,
> never quitting,
> never saying 'die', and
> never taking 'no' for an answer"

https://mvp.microsoft.com/en-us/PublicProfile/5001695
https://www.linkedin.com/in/clintonwyckoff/
https://twitter.com/ClintWyckoff
Clint: David's Book Reviews, notes and videos on DavidPLundell.com

Seven Day Wonder, Humbled

One day, about a year after we had doubled the size of the consulting practice I led (and a short while after I had written the first ever book on the Microsoft product in which my team specialized), my manager called me into his office.

"Dude, you're letting the cracks show!"

He was worried about me. As I excelled in my career, I would keep saying yes and take on more and more. On occasion that resulted in a few items slipping through the cracks (some more noticeable than others).

But, I really was great at time management … up to a point

I had always worked hard and excelled. I was a National Merit Scholar, and was the Arizona AP Scholar, which meant I passed more Advanced Placement exams with better scores than any other boy in the class of 1993 in all of Arizona. I did that while lettering in Soccer and Football, working for my Dad's software company, earning the Eagle Scout Rank (Boy Scouts of America's highest rank), having an active dating life, serving in church youth leadership roles, and even taking on a small role in student government. My mother even called me "a seven-day wonder," as in, "I wonder how you fit it all into the seven days of the week." I was one of the best at maximizing the effectiveness of my time. I had even used Franklin Covey Planners for years before Microsoft Outlook became an effective tool.

In school, where my goal was to learn as much as possible and earn just above 90% for an A (sometimes I was ok with a B), it wasn't a problem to let an item here or there slip through the cracks. My high school teachers and college professors didn't really care if I missed one or two homework assignments. However, you can't always prioritize that way at work – or, more correctly, you cannot take it as a given; you have to communicate it and negotiate it.

How did I take it?

Even though I had written two books, had a Bachelor's in Computer Engineering, a Master's in Business Administration, was a Microsoft MVP, and had doubled the size of our Identity Management practice, my supervisor was concerned about the slippages – and I agreed.

He recommended that I read and implement the practices detailed in a book called Take Back Your Life with Outlook 2007, by Sally McGhee and John Wittry.

What did I do?

I took his advice. I read the book, I put it into practice (not perfectly, but that's why it is called practice), and as a result a weakness became a strength. I learned how to track my commitments in such a way that I could see when I was getting too busy and then decline new commitments, or if I couldn't decline them, get the higher authority to pick which commitment to drop. I discovered the ability to say, "No," then to follow that up with "If you absolutely need me to do this, which other commitment do you want to renegotiate for me?" Admittedly, this newfound skill *did* sometimes lead to my manager's consternation, but I nonetheless regained a measure of control over my life.

I also proceeded to teach these things to my team, and of course I also recommended that they too should "Take Back [their Lives] with Outlook" and buy that book.

> "I had to humble myself and be willing to be taught
> in an area where I already felt I was one of the best."

It wasn't easy. I could have blamed my manager, or the many other coworkers that imposed on my time. I could have gotten mad, pointed to my accomplishments, and told him to shove off. I could have told him that I was shoving off (aka quitting). Instead, I had to humble myself and be willing to be taught in an area where I already felt I was one of the best.

Microsoft MVPs

Sometimes, listening to the coach has a direct impact on your life. For Argentinian Pablo Di Loreto, a friend told him of the MVP program, and encouraged him to focus his blogging and contributions so that he could be recognized as an MVP and gain more clout to be able to help more people. His director at work, also then an MVP, encouraged this as well, knowing that it would make Pablo more valuable to clients and teammates.

Microsoft MVP Clint Wyckoff benefitted from the mentoring of Dave and Cristal Kawula, two Canadian MVPs who taught him the art of blogging and brought him to edit and contribute to a book wherein they spearheaded an ensemble effort to document and describe an exciting new Microsoft Cloud Product -- Storage Spaces Direct. Dave and Cristal, what a great job!

Gretchen (Opferkew) Mann dedicates herself to being a good coach, mentoring the teammates she manages, having one-on-one conversations to guide them on their career paths, and helping them develop their strengths and shore up their weaknesses.

Pablo Ariel Di Loreto

Argentina

MVP 2014 – Present

Category: Azure, Windows and

Devices for IT

In 2017 Pablo was a rare double category Microsoft MVP, awarded for both "Azure" and "Windows and Devices for IT."

He started working in the technology industry at the age of sixteen. His friend Erica told him about the Microsoft MVP program and encouraged him to focus his contributions to the field in more meaningful and immediately effective ways. Pablo wrote articles and presented remotely via webcasts and in person, including special events in Argentina.

Pablo has made it one of his goals in life to teach others, and this passion for teaching and helping others has fueled his success.

Pablo's director at Emiliano (his employer) was previously an MVP, and gave Pablo the opportunity to shine by encouraging him to leverage his extensive experience and skills to lift up himself and others.

He claims his self-improvement program is very Argentinian. It certainly displays a great deal of humility and teachability. One of his mottos is: "Don't believe you know everything. Always orient towards the fountain of all knowledge. Always analyze; Always ask if you don't understand."

> "Don't believe you know everything.
> Always orient towards the fountain of all knowledge.
> Always analyze;
> Always ask if you don't understand."

https://www.linkedin.com/in/pablodiloreto/
https://mvp.microsoft.com/en-us/PublicProfile/5000700
Pablo: David's notes and videos on DavidPLundell.com

When is it best not to Listen to the Coach? (Steve Young)

"Everyone laughed." (Steve Young BYU's All-American QB, 1984).

"That guys sucks!" (Young S. &., 2016).

"He can't throw!" (Young S. &., 2016).

These were the initial impressions of some of Steve Young's teammates at Brigham Young University (BYU). After these first few embarrassing practices, the Quarterbacks Coach, Doug Scovil, quickly and bluntly dismissed the 8th string QB to the practice squad, proclaiming, "I will not coach a lefty," and expressing his thoughts that lefties shouldn't be Quarterbacks (KSL, 2016).

Given Steve's place in both the BYU Hall of Fame and in the NFL Hall of Fame, it is easy to use hindsight to say that Doug Scovil was wrong – very wrong! But who knew that at the time? In his four seasons at BYU, Scovil had coached three All-American Quarterbacks: Gifford Nielsen, Marc Wilson, and Jim McMahon (76-77, 79-80), the first two of whom were already in the NFL at the time. If anyone knew what made a good quarterback, it would have been Doug Scovil. Even the head coach, Lavell Edwards, wanted to move Young to defense, noting, "I think we have our quarterbacks … we need defensive backs" (Steve Young BYU's All-American QB, 1984).

We all have heard the singers on the original American Idol who sounded terrible and refused to give up when Simon Cowell was cruel in an attempt to be kind and save them from wasting their lives chasing dreams that won't happen. How did Steve know that he would prove Scovil wrong and show the world that he wasn't like those singers?

For one thing, Steve said that his coach's "statement actually motivated me. Despite all of my insecurities, I was attracted to the impossible" (Young S. &., 2016). For another, he had never been taught how to do the things that Doug Scovil was asking of him. Scovil never really gave him a chance to learn how to be a passing quarterback; instead he expected him to already know it. Scovil was like a boss that gives up on the new hire because he hasn't trained him yet! Instead of asking himself how he could develop Young (with his obvious speed and intelligence) into a great quarterback, he looked at all of his flaws (left-handed, doesn't know how to do a drop back, etc.) and dismissed him.

Be respectful, but question it!

If the coach's comments and advice aren't constructive and don't give you a way to improve, then by all means you should question it! However, do so first in the privacy of your own mind and/or with trusted advisors. Did the coach really have a chance to judge my skills fairly? Can I get a second opinion? Is that something that I can improve, or have I already given it my best shot? Do I have the raw talents that can be refined into the necessary well-honed skills? Do I have the work ethic to make it happen? Can I develop that ethic? What help and support do I need? Sometimes, people criticize based on what is missing instead of seeing the potential. In those cases, it is up to you to fill in the rest of the picture for them.

When Steve had coaches that evaluated him fairly and gave him constructive feedback, he listened and he learned.

8th String Quarterback to Hall of Famer

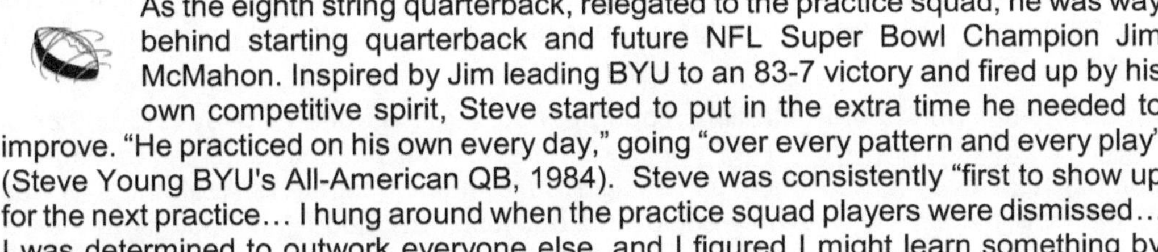As the eighth string quarterback, relegated to the practice squad, he was way behind starting quarterback and future NFL Super Bowl Champion Jim McMahon. Inspired by Jim leading BYU to an 83-7 victory and fired up by his own competitive spirit, Steve started to put in the extra time he needed to improve. "He practiced on his own every day," going "over every pattern and every play" (Steve Young BYU's All-American QB, 1984). Steve was consistently "first to show up for the next practice… I hung around when the practice squad players were dismissed… I was determined to outwork everyone else, and I figured I might learn something by watching McMahon" (Young S. &., 2016).

Young started imitating McMahon and "overnight … could throw the ball with pinpoint accuracy and a lot of power." After the season was over Steve began drilling himself in the key skills. "From the beginning of January to the end of February, I threw more than 10,000 spirals. Over and over again. And then some. My arm hurt. But I wanted to be a quarterback" (Young S. &., 2016).

> "From the beginning of January to the end of February, I threw more than 10,000 spirals."
> – Steve Young, describing his refocused dedication after his freshman season.

Eventually Coach Scovil left, and Ted Tollner, the new quarterbacks coach, saw Steve's new and improved skills. As a result, "Tollner told Coach Edwards 'I don't think we should move Steve,'" (Steve Young BYU's All-American QB, 1984). "Without [that year with] Ted, I probably would have never played quarterback at BYU" (Young S. &., 2016).

The combination of a graduation, a transfer, and outworking the others allowed Steve to rise from the depths and become Number Two, backing up Jim McMahon himself.

His next quarterbacks coach, Mike Holmgren, helped him complete his transition from a run first quarterback to one that passes first. Steve's "biggest problem was patience… a tendency to flee the pocket at the first sign of pressure… [he] wasn't giving [his] receivers enough time to get open on the deep routes" (Young S. &., 2016).

In the pros, Young went through some tumultuous times in the now defunct USFL, and then spent two years with the Tampa Buccaneers, where he was sacked 68 times in 17 games. Finally, 49ers Head Coach Bill Walsh, considered by many to be the greatest head coach ever, brought Steve Young to San Francisco. As Steve told our youth group at church in 1990, he was brought in to take over for a "a guy who had a bad back [Joe Montana]." That's not exactly how it worked out, at least initially. Joe Montana went on to be the starter for four more seasons, winning two more Super Bowls.

During this period of frustration, Young encountered Stephen Covey (the author of <u>The 7 Habits of Highly Effective People</u>) on a flight. After patiently listening to Young's complaints, Covey turned Steve's thinking around, helping him to realize that "[he] was in the one place… where [he] could find out just how good [he could] get," as a quarterback (Young S. &., 2016).

Also, during that time, Young learned more about quarterbacking from Walsh than he ever thought there was to know. Walsh told him that the key to being a great passer was to "'just follow the directions," and that "the footwork" would "tell you the timing…when to deliver the football [and] to [whom]." Young's initial reaction was to say "What?!" At first, he couldn't believe it. He had been an All-American QB at BYU (sometimes known as Pass U because of how often they passed the ball), and he had already played for two other professional teams (the now defunct USFL's LA Express and the NFL's Tampa Bay Buccaneers). He had never heard anything so preposterous. But Steve listened to his coach. As a result, he "started to learn the footwork of the West Coast Offense" -- an offense that, with its "short passing game, [was] replicating the efficiency and the security of a running game… that's what changed things" (NFL Network, 2015).

Personal value of Listening to the Coach

I have often heard that the ritual of the annual performance reviews is more of an exercise in beating you down just enough to justify only giving you a small raise, but not so small that you want to leave. That's not really the coaching I am talking about. Although many good managers do their best to use these reviews to inspire, the coaching that really makes a difference happens monthly, weekly, and even daily. Every single one of my managers and leaders had something valuable for me to learn. Often, the coach can see past our blind spots and hold up a mirror to what we need to be seeing but usually are not.

If you don't think that coaches might be of value to you, pause for a second and consider how much professional coaches get paid!

How can I listen better?

Below is my diagram for listening. First, we hear. Then, we comprehend. Next, we consider in whole or in part. Finally, we can analyze what has been said in order to find the appropriate parts upon which to act.

5 The Process of Listening

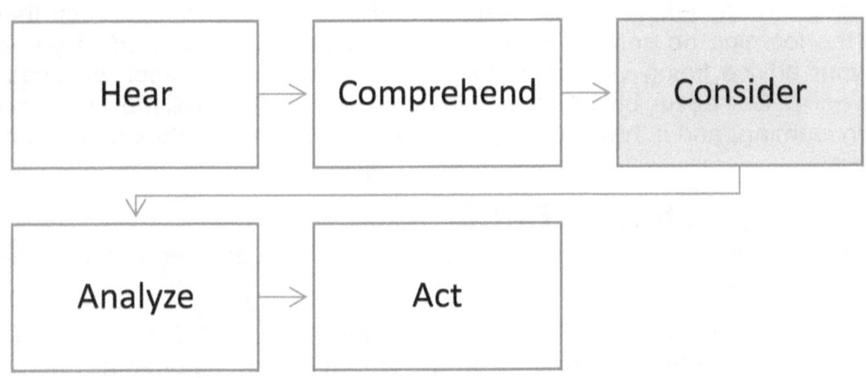

All too often, we fail to give adequate consideration to feedback that hurts or requires growth on our part. To combat this very natural tendency, I will refer to one of the most impactful business books I have ever read, Crucial Conversations. In it, the authors ask us to pay careful attention to the stories we tell ourselves. Have we made ourselves victims? Have we turned someone else into the villain? Have we given up all control and made ourselves helpless? Learning can be hard, especially when we must face the hard truth that sometimes we aren't as noble in our intentions or as skilled in our tasks as we imagined ourselves to be. The dangerous thing about these stories is that we tell them to make ourselves feel good so we don't have to go through the pain of learning and improving. Again and again, without fail, when a project has delays, goes overbudget, or just outright fails, watch and these three types of stories will appear in your mind and on the lips of others (Patterson, Grenny, McMillan, & Switzler, 2002).

Of course, there are others involved that also need to learn and improve. This also shouldn't be taken to suggest that there aren't true victim stories. However, we must be honest in assessing every stumble, and willing to face the causes, even when some of the causes of failure might be our own shortcomings and blind spots. There is ALWAYS something to learn.

As an example, some years ago someone broke into our car while we were at church. The thieves found our address in the glove box (thank you state mandated car registration for printing the address on the form) and took our garage door remote. They then burgled our house, taking documents, cash (from a car we just sold), a video camera (yup, back before everyone had a phone with them built in), and a laptop computer. We truly were victimized. And yet even in this story we still had things to learn. I had left the car door unlocked. We also learned that removable garage door remotes leave you vulnerable to this kind of theft. We learned. I started making sure I locked the door each time I left my car, and we switched to key chain remotes that we could carry with us and not leave in the car.

You also need to be cautious about trying to push the learning on others. You may see someone else going through a similar experience. Before swooping in with your wisdom to save the day consider their feelings and the best way to approach them. Don't push the learning on someone else who has just been victimized. If you do, instead of your advice being viewed as helpful you could find yourself accused of blaming the victim. Be helpful, but be patient. In due time, the victim will most likely seek out their own learning, and if they know you remain their true friend they might turn to you for advice.

Action Plan: Listening Better

Right now, think of the last time you complained about something major. Write it down, here or in a separate notebook:

- Ask yourself, "How have I contributed to this problem?" Dig deep and be honest. Again, write your answers down, no matter how big or small the detail may be.

- If you blamed someone else, ask yourself, "If I assumed they had reasonable and decent intentions, why might they have done this?" They may or may not have had decent intentions, and they may or may not have been acting rationally, but give it a try. Once more, please write it down.

- Follow the advice from <u>Crucial Conversations</u> and ask yourself, "What do I really want out of this relationship? What would I do right now if I really wanted these results?" (Patterson, Grenny, McMillan, & Switzler, 2002). Please write down your plan. Be sure to include what the problem is, what results you are seeking, what you will do, when you will do it, how you will do it, and how you will measure your progress.

Ultimately, we can only control ourselves. When it comes to others, we can only invite them to learn and to lead by example.

- To whose advice should I listen? Here is a good litmus test for advice:
  - Is the advice honest? Did the giver of the advice really have a chance to evaluate my abilities? Does the advice give me a way to improve?

- In what ways could my manager serve as a coach?

- How can I find and cultivate a coach or a mentor?

Look for someone whom you admire with the skills you hope to learn or someone who excels at asking thought provoking questions. Look at those with whom you already associate. You may need to join a club, or an open source project, or found a community effort, or change jobs, in order to be able to associate with this person. Alternatively, you might need to initiate some of the aforementioned projects to even become aware of some of these folks.

- Who could possibly serve as my coach or mentor?

- How should I use coaches that I don't pay for without abusing the privilege?
    1) Meet with them during meals or other times when they can talk without taking away from their valuable time. You should consider making the meal your treat.
    2) Approach them with well thought out questions rather than whiny complaints.
        a. Instead of, "Oh I hate my boss, he is such a micro manager," try, "Hey, I need some help figuring out how to best work with my boss. On a number of occasions, she seems to micromanage me and that frustrates me. What can I do to inspire her trust? Is there some other problem I am not aware of affecting this relationship?"
    3) Explain what you hope to gain from the conversation. Do you want your coach to:
        a. Point you towards a resource?
        b. Help you understand something better?
        c. Be a mirror to help you understand yourself?
        d. Something entirely different?

    Make sure you are clear about your issue and the resolution you are seeking. Be on the same page as your coach!

- When should I pay for a coach?

I have never paid for a coach, except indirectly (in sports where someone else paid their salaries, or at work where a manager or more senior teammate imparted wisdom). However, one of my brothers is contemplating a massive career change and he has hired a coach to assist him with this transition. He took this route because he feels like he will be more successful if he could call on her when he needs her guidance and not just when it was convenient for a friend to get together for the occasional lunch. A good rule of thumb is that you should consider a financial arrangement with your coach if:

1) You need so much of their time that they should charge you money to offset the loss of their time and energy.
2) You need access to them on *your* schedule and not just at their convenience.

I suppose the editor I hired for this book is also acting like a coach, giving me guidance and feedback on my writing. As I think about it, the two criteria above match exactly why I hired an editor rather than getting some free reviews/edits done by friends (the route I took with one of my technical books).

- How do I find a good coach to hire?
    - Look for an MVP (or someone like an MVP in your field).
    - Check their reviews and references.
    - Ask yourself honestly, "Can you trust them?"

Chapter 4: Work through injuries and challenges (Perseverance)

What a Funk for the Murph!

 Dale Murphy had only one hit his first season of Little League baseball. Yes, the man who at age 27 became the youngest player in the major leagues to ever win back to back MVP awards only had one hit his first season of little league. But he had fun anyway and didn't even really notice and went on to have a very successful amateur career (Wolsey, 1985).

His professional career began in 1974, when the Atlanta Braves drafted him in the first round with the 5th overall pick. They selected him for his defensive prowess as a catcher. After making the Southern League all-star team (a minor league) in 1976 (Schlossberg, 2010), he got a taste of the big leagues, getting called up in September of that year. After a reasonably strong defensive performance (he threw out 9 of the 30 baserunners trying to steal a base and only committed 3 errors in 116 chances, 2.59%, over 19 games) he was expected to win the starting job as the Braves catcher. But the scouts never thought that he would grow to be a great hitter or hit lots of home runs. They wanted him mainly for his defensive abilities.

No one will steal Centerfield on you

Then, during spring training in 1977, he missed his throw to second base when trying to stop someone from stealing. The next day against the Yankees he overthrew second, putting the ball into centerfield. His father reportedly remarked that no one would be able to steal centerfield on him. Even worse, "later that year he twice plunked his own pitcher in the back on throws to second" (Demak, 1991). His manager sent him back down to the minor leagues, where he settled down a little, making only 12 errors at catcher in 562 chances, 2.14%, over 90 games. While in the minors he also got a taste of playing first base. When he got called up to the Majors again, his woes returned. He made 6 errors in 113 chances, 5.31% over 18 games (by comparison, playing in the 1974 rookie league he made 7 errors in 424 chances, 1.65%, over the course of 52 games).

"Later that year he twice plunked his own **pitcher in the back on throws to second.**"
– Sportswriter Richard Demak, on Dale Murphy's sudden struggles at catcher

---

What happened?

How do you go from being one of the top defensive prospects at catcher to beaning your own pitcher, and having trouble getting the ball 60 feet back to the pitcher?

Murphy explained, "Your mind won't let your natural abilities flow… you start thinking, 'Where am I throwing?' … instead of just throwing." This sounds like a classic case of the Yips – where, "Your mind starts working against you" (Demak, 1991).

Was there a Silver Lining?

After being sent back down to the minor leagues in 1977, Dale hit 22 home runs and 142 hits out of 466 at-bats for a .305 batting average. When he was called back up to the Majors in September, suddenly he was hitting major league pitching and doing it quite well, with 2 home runs, 14 runs batted in, and 24 hits out of 76 at bats, for a solid .316 average (Dale Murphy, 2018). Suddenly, his defensive performance at catcher wasn't all that important.

Dale's struggles with his original claim to fame may have allowed his even more impressive talent of hitting home runs to shine and, as we shall soon see, extended his career.

Where to put the Murph?

In 1978 and 1979 Dale's manager Bobby Cox tried him at first base as well as catcher, but his defense was terrible. He racked up 35 errors in 1,991 chances at first base and 8 errors in 246 chances at catcher, 3.25%. In 1978 he "led" all first baseman in the league with 20 errors (NOT the category in which you want to lead the league!). One of the only reasons he didn't top the league in 1979 was because he played 55 fewer games at first base that season. However, even with a lower number of games at the position, he still came within 2 errors of tying for the lead. His hitting slumped to .226 in 1978, but he hit 23 home runs. In 1979 he rebounded to hit .276 with 21 home runs.

After the 1979 season, manager Bobby Cox solved the quandary when he moved him from playing in the infield to playing in the outfield. After a couple of years, he became so good at the outfield that in 1982, Dale won the Golden Glove as one of the top three defensive outfielders in the league. He won the Golden Glove again in 1983, 1984, 1985 and 1986!

"But anyone who saw him [play catcher] could not have imagined the remarkable transition. 'I couldn't throw, and it was very frustrating,' admitted Murphy... 'I had all this God-given talent, and all of a sudden I couldn't play. I tried to keep it in perspective and not let it affect my relationships with people'" (Schlossberg, 2010).

Further Silver Lining

The move to the outfield certainly extended his career. Playing catcher is notoriously tough on the knees, and as a result, catchers tend to have shorter careers. Outfielders, on the other hand, don't usually have as many knee problems. (Eventually, though, Dale's knee problems did slow him down later in his career.)

More serious woes

Dale and his wife Nancy have eight children – no, that's not the woes to which I refer. Their second child, Travis, has Rubinstein-Taybi Syndrome, which retards physical and mental development. They also lost a child during pregnancy. Regarding his second child, Dale has said, "I'm grateful to Heavenly Father that if Travis had to be born with this problem, he came to us, so we could give him the medical help he needs" (Wolsey, 1985). You can see how his attitude has a big impact on his family and his career.

Octavio Hernandez

Los Angeles, CA, USA

MVP 2004-2010

Category: C#

Octavio's story starts in Cuba, his native country. In 1992 Cuba was decidedly NOT the land of opportunity, so at age 32, Octavio made the most difficult decision of his life and fearlessly put it into action – he left Cuba, and his post as Assistant Professor at the Faculty of Mathematics and Computer Science of the Havana University, to relocate to Spain. There, he found work as a consultant and as a professor of programming languages. As Octavio gave more presentations and wrote more and more articles, he eventually caught someone's eye at Microsoft (perhaps it was another MVP). He was nominated in 2004 and joined the roster of Microsoft MVPs.

> "At age 32, Octavio made the most difficult decision of his life and fearlessly put it into action – he left Cuba"

In 2007, Octavio wrote a book on a language that was rising rapidly in popularity, LINQ. This was a special accomplishment for Octavio because he has always had a great love for teaching.

In 2010, he moved to Los Angeles, and with the change in job and surroundings he stopped making as many contributions to the community and was not renewed for the MVP Program.

Outside of the technical world, Octavio has made valuable contributions in the most important place – the home. He has poured sweat, joy and tears into raising his two kids, the youngest of whom will become a university graduate in 2018.

https://mvp.microsoft.com/en-us/PublicProfile/9597
https://www.linkedin.com/in/octaviohernandez/
Octavio: David's Book Reviews, notes and videos on DavidPLundell.com

Bell Rung (Sid the Kid Crosby)

Over the span of five short days in early January 2011, Sid "the kid" Crosby "suffered hits to his head from Dave Steckel and Victor Hedman, respectively" (Sidney Crosby, n.d.). He missed the 2nd half of the 2010-2011 season, three quarters of the next season (2011-2012), and about half of the following season (2012-2013). "There were some dark days when the thought he may never play hockey again at the professional level entered his mind" (Hargreaves, 2013).

Without a definite timeframe to follow, Crosby explained the challenge of recovering from a concussion by explaining that "you feel like you're getting better" and then "one day and you're back to where you started. It's a frustrating injury" (Hargreaves, 2013). Crosby had a long and uncertain road to recovery.

How did he deal with the uncertainty?

Christian Marin wrote an article in September of 2011, a time when no one knew when or if Crosby would be able to return to professional hockey, noting that "Although there … is no time table, … Crosby is staying active and remaining the [MVP] that he is off the ice" by helping "small communities and charities." Marin opined that he was "Sending a hidden message" (perhaps an even more important message) "to children everywhere that it is alright for them to sit the next one out if they are injured, especially if the injury is a concussion." This message is even more effective to the youth because Crosby "is the poster boy for hard work and perseverance, not just hockey and the NHL" (Marin, 2011).

"Forget yourself and serve others."

My worries

Although it seems silly now, during my first semester of college in the fall of 1993, I was really worried about school and (of course!) whether a girl liked me or not. As I struggled with these worries, a completely new thought entered my head: "Forget yourself and serve others." As I looked around my apartment I noticed I had the raw materials to brighten the day for some friends. I had a tank of helium and some balloons (both were left over from a recently completed engineering class project). So armed, I wrote inspirational messages for twelve friends, attached them to the helium filled balloons, and dropped them off at their apartments and dorms. One friend noted that she was so stressed and crushed after a math mid-term exam that when she saw the balloon it really lifted her spirits knowing that someone else cared. That act of service didn't make my problems disappear, but I felt good, and as a result my problems didn't seem as big. Consequently, my worries diminished. Service really *does* have its own rewards.

Kathy Jacobs
El Monte, CA, USA

MVP 2003 – 2012

Category: PowerPoint & OneNote

Claiming to have the "the word 'sucker' stamped on [her] forehead," Kathy's business card reads, "Serial Volunteer." She gets a thrill out of "breaking the code" and finding hidden features and bugs to help people work around their problems. Her reward for her MVP mindset of service is that by "doing something that mattered for someone else, [it] helped [her] understand that [she] was better than [she] thought [she] was."

Before facing some severe health challenges, Kathy was one of the busiest MVPs, answering forum questions, speaking at (and organizing) various conferences, leading national user group organizations, and speaking in small user group venues. On three occasions she delivered 30 presentations in 21 days across Phoenix at various user groups. She has also written or co-authored at least four books.

Kathy underwent six knee surgeries in five years, but the encouragement she received from her fellow MVPs kept her going and did not slow her down. Essentially, the message she received was, "We don't care that the knees are slowing you down; come play with us." These friendships and associations got her and her husband through some tough times, as more than once they lost everything while working for various startups.

Kathy says that beta testing is a great way to keep up with a new product and presenting on the product ensures that you can explain it to others.

She volunteered many years with Brownies and Girl Scouts. She and her husband (the "Serial Volunteer" accomplice) also managed the technical lighting and sound for a theater in Rochester.

To those that complain they lack the time, Kathy says, "Do it!" and points out that there are questions on many social media platforms that go unanswered. Go help someone, she advises, noting: "It's addicting."

https://www.linkedin.com/in/callkathy/
https://mvp.microsoft.com/en-us/PublicProfile/8664
Kathy: David's Book Reviews, Notes and Videos on DavidPLundell.com

What me worry? (Steve Young)

To most people, Steve Young has always seemed to have it all. As a junior in high school he was the starting quarterback, the basketball team's starting point guard, and the ace of the baseball team's pitching staff – not to mention perfect grades, perfect attendance (at both church *and* school), and he was dating the head cheerleader. Good grief! Yet, in an interview with Peter King as he was promoting his autobiography, Behind the Spiral, he revealed how we he was haunted by "incredible separation anxiety" to the point where he didn't ever "do sleep overs" as a kid and elaborated how that morphed into severe performance anxiety (Young S. , Steve Young Talks Separation Anxiety, Relationship with Joe Montana, 2016).

According to the anxiety.org website, "Separation anxiety disorder describes an individual's feelings of persistent and excessive anxiety related to … separation from an attachment figure." People so afflicted "experience overwhelming distress and anxiety when separated from their attachment figure." For Steve the attachment figures seemed to be his parents.

"Experience overwhelming distress and anxiety"

In his autobiography, Steve explained how his acute separation anxiety disorder created a conflict. At BYU, even after becoming the starting quarterback, he felt "lonely and … desperately wanted to catch the next flight back [home]. *But* [he] also wanted to prove that [he] could be great," at BYU (Young S. &., 2016) (emphasis added).

Leading into his first home start for BYU and filling in for the amazing but injured Jim McMahon, Young wasn't worried about getting tackled or hurt, but rather about losing the game and thereby ending the "sixteen-game winning streak" and disappointing everyone: fans, alumni, and church members around the world (BYU is a private school owned by the Church of Jesus Christ of Latter Day Saints, sometimes nicknamed the LDS church or Mormon church, and as a result it has a worldwide fan base). Reflecting back on this time he noted, "Anxiety comes from deep within your body, and when it flows out it's almost impossible to control on your own" (Young S. &., 2016). All of that was piled on Steve as a nineteen-year-old kid.

In a recent interview Steve described the worst way this anxiety would manifest before games. "You wake up … and you have this dread, like, 'Ohhhh not another one'" (Young S. , Steve Young's mental struggle off the playing field, 2017).

David P Lundell

Mo' Money, Mo' Problems or the $40 Million Dollar Man

The pressures on him only intensified as a pro, especially when he passed over the $3.5 million in unguaranteed money from the Cincinnati Bengals of the NFL to became the "$40 million-dollar man" in 1984 by signing a four year commitment to play for the LA Express of the USFL – a short-lived league that tried and failed to compete with the NFL (Breech, 2013).

In contrast, later that same year, quarterback Warren Moon (coming to the NFL from the Canadian Football League (CFL) as a free agent after leading his team to five straight championships and twice earning the CFL MVP award) was offered a five-year contract: $4.5 million as a signing bonus and $1 million in total salary over the five years for a total worth of $5.5 million dollars to join the NFL's then Houston Oilers (now the Tennessee Titans).

According to Steve's agent, "Money never was his motivation" for joining the LA Express. It was to "get better quarterback coaching and more opportunity to play" (ThePostGame Staff, 2013). Plus, the money wasn't as great as it seemed.

While the $40 million dollars made great headlines for the upstart league, his new team, and his agent, the reality is that Steve was offered $4 million in a signing bonus and few hundred thousand a year in annual salary plus a choice between about $1 million in upfront money or an almost $35 million 40-year annuity (Breech, 2013).

The PostGame Staff (ThePostGame Staff, 2013) and Fox Sports (Fox Sports, 2013) have said that the $40 million-dollar contract from 1984 would be worth a staggering $90-100 million dollars in today's dollars (after being adjusted for inflation), but that just isn't true. The value of the $40 million-dollar contract in 1984 dollars wasn't even $40 million dollars, but closer to $6 million dollars - MUCH closer to the $5.5 million that Warren Moon agreed to with the Oilers.

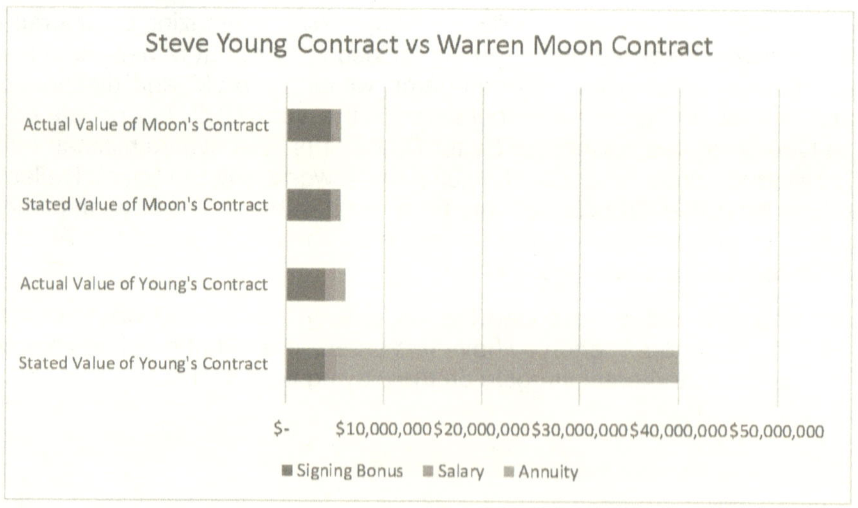

Six million dollars was quite fitting since according to the LA Express Wikipedia article Lee Majors (the actor who starred in the Six Million Dollar Man television show) had become part owner of the team in the prior year.

How was $40 Million really only $6 Million?

If you don't care how then skip this next paragraph.

The biggest part of the contract, about $35 million dollars, was the annuity which would have started paying in 1989 and kept paying in slowly increasing annual amounts until 2027. Since money to be paid in the future is worth less than money to be paid today, we must discount the value of future money. How do we know how much the annuity was worth? In 1984, Steve was offered a choice between the annuity and around $1 million dollars in cash, so we can figure that the annuity was worth about $1 Million dollars in 1984. Add that to his signing bonus of $4 million and his guaranteed salary for four years (which totaled $1.21 million), then discount that to $1.06 million (because most of that was future money), and you get just over $6 million dollars, which was still a lot of money in 1984. Adjusted for inflation, I would estimate the contract to be worth $14 Million in 2018 dollars.

Pressure

The point is that signing what was not only hailed as the biggest pro sports contract ever, but a contract that seemed to dwarf every other pro sports contract in existence, hung these enormous expectations on Steve, which "tormented" him (Young S. , Steve Young's mental struggle off the playing field, 2017).

> "Signing … a contract that seemed to dwarf every other pro sports contract in existence, hung these enormous expectations"

Steve was quite aware that he had great gifts that he, his coaches, and his teammates had honed well. He was "the fastest quarterback in the NFL, [and could] hit the whiskers on a cat with a football from a distance of forty yards." In addition to his physical abilities, he "has a photographic memory …[and] can visualize what everyone in the huddle is supposed to do on each of the hundreds of plays in [the] playbook" (Young S. &., 2016).

Yet with all of that going for him, during the time leading up to each game he was beset by anxiety. In those moments, Steve admitted that his thoughts were simply, "I don't want to get out of bed" (Young S. &., 2016). I think we all have had some bad days where we don't want to get out of bed, but this was before every single game and wasn't tied to a tragedy or even anything bad happening, although a negative experience could exacerbate the problem.

Similar to the paradox he experienced in college, Young reflected "I [longed] to be the best quarterback in the NFL. I [dreaded] being the best quarterback in the NFL" (Young S. &., 2016).

Microsoft MVPs

Ten years prior to our interview, 28-year-old Clint Wyckoff was diagnosed with cancer. He credits his "never quit, never say die, never take no for an answer" attitude with helping him persevere through the illness and treatment. He noted that it made him a better parent and helps him to instill values in his kids.

Kathy Jacobs had six knee surgeries in five years.

Serial volunteer and former MVP Kathy Jacobs had six knee surgeries in five years and is medically retired. Even today she walks with the support of a cane. As her injuries afflicted her and she endured countless surgeries, she felt hopeless, even believing that she "couldn't do anything." She couldn't deliver technical training sessions because the doctors didn't want her to sit down, but other people her life (MVPs and more) said "we don't care [about the injuries], come and play with us." She mentioned an occasion where she was invited to train and speak, and was worried about sitting for too long *and* having to stand for too long. The event organizer told her that she could assume whatever positions would help her. More than once she and her husband "lost everything" financially while "working for startups that crashed." She credits the friends she has made in the MVP program with helping her pull through. Her love for this program and the people in it is quite evident as she started a Facebook group for MVP's and MVP Alumni. She overcame these challenges with help from friends and by finding ways to serve.

After 10 years in the Canadian Armed Forces,
Rob Prouse realized he had to reinvent himself.

Over ten years and attending seven schools, Gretchen (Opferkew) Mann finally achieved her goal of earning a college degree. As a young adult she spent a year as a non-profit worker in Africa. She realized how much she wanted to help the world become a better place, and determined to earn a degree in counseling. Her focus then shifted to management of non-profits. For ten years she worked and made her way into

Information Technology, and upon graduation she realized that she was already making the world a better place using the technology skills she developed along the way.

Rob Prouse's first career was in the military. Leaving after ten years in the Canadian Armed Forces, he realized he had to reinvent himself. He told me how he was learning programming and how he was able to break through the "no experience barrier." He "walked into a game development company" and "convinced them to take a chance on [him]" by offering to work for free for six months. After his six month "internship," they gave him a decent wage. Additionally, Rob is very introverted and he has had to learn to develop his communication skills, recognizing that a key function of a development lead is "to talk to people and understand requirements and business problems."

Rob Richardson also faced a career pivot when he "looked around" at work and "realized that [he] had two more degrees than everyone else" and was working on "proprietary software" with nowhere to go from there. Following this realization, Rob began retraining himself on other technologies. Rob stresses that while many may benefit from managers serving as coaches or others as mentors, ultimately you and you alone are in charge of your own career.

Hal Hostetler of Tucson explains that after getting older and having knee surgery and back problems, he was forcibly medically retired. Despite that, he continues his volunteer work, answering questions about Microsoft technology and HAM and broadcast radio work, saying that his "retirement" leaves him with "more time for the newsgroups!"

Jason Brimhall's LinkedIn profile reveals that he started college in 1996 at Utah State University, earned an Associates in Network Administration in 2003 from Western Governors University, and earned his Bachelors of Science in Business Information Systems from Utah State University in 2008. Why twelve years for a bachelor's? Not from a lack of intelligence, but probably from raising and supporting a family. Despite his obstacles and responsibilities, with perseverance and hard work he was able to accomplish his goal of earning a degree.

> "Imagine leaving your home country to start all over
> again - twice!"

Imagine leaving your home country to start all over again - twice! Former Microsoft MVP Octavio Hernandez Leal left Cuba at age 32, leaving behind his assistant professorship at Havana University to relocate to Spain in search of freedom and opportunity. He found work doing IT consulting and teaching computer programming. Eventually, his articles and speaking garnered him a nomination for MVP. He repeated the process in 2010 (albeit a little less dramatically this time), moving from Spain to the United States and sunny Los Angeles, California.

Insult and Injury (Steve Nash)

While Steve Nash had plenty of supporters, there were even more detractors. "People have always told me that I'd fall on my face, that I wouldn't make it this far. But here I am" (McCallum, 2006). In High School he "found it difficult to balance school and sports" (Bailey, 2007), so his parents transferred him to a new school and he had to sit out a year. As discussed earlier, he used that time to hone his skills.

Only one college, Santa Clara University, even bothered to recruit him for Basketball (Feschuk, 2014).

On top of the lack of attention, Nash developed a medical condition called Spondylolisthesis (a slipped or displaced vertebrae). Consequently, during games when Steve was not on the court he would lie down on his back. This would help him keep his back muscles loose and not stiffen up (McCallum, 2006).

Wasn't a Prospect (Ben Zobrist)

Like Nash, Zobrist didn't get a lot of attention coming out of high school. He was "from a small town," and he wasn't a hot "prospect [like] a lot of these guys were going through the minor leagues." Instead he went to small Christian universities and finally got "drafted as a senior in college." When he got to the major leagues, he explained that "I found things that worked for me to help me be valuable to the teams I was on."

Playing a sport where a 30% success rate for a hitter is considered great, Ben remarked that in baseball, "We fail a lot. We have to learn how to deal with [it] as best we can and keep coming back for more." He truly feels that "perseverance … is very important to atmosphere and attitude" for the "whole team.'

"We fail a lot. We have to learn
how to deal with [it] as best we can
and keep coming back for more."
– Ben Zobrist

Won the World Series, what's next? Depression!

Ben shared with me that he has "been through depression a couple of different times," including right after he "won the MVP in the World Series." He notes that with "the pressure of a high-profile job," with its "highs and lows," that "if you don't take care of your health" you can end up in a "tough place" emotionally when "it all goes away quickly." Ben reflected that "some of those moments that have been the darkest and most difficult times of my life have also helped me have a new appreciation for [our humanity]." Ben wisely observed that "any person... high profile" or otherwise, "is a human being first," and "employee or player second." Zobrist is definitely "passionate about trying to help people understand and navigate those pressures."

When Ben retires in a few years, I can easily envision his transformation into a very successful career and life coach for high-profile, high-pressure people. He didn't share his post baseball plans, so I thought I would offer it up as a possibility. (Ben, I hope you're listening!)

Personal Value of getting back in the game

Eventually, we all retire. Dale Murphy retired after knee problems reduced his performance significantly. Steve Young retired after suffering several concussions. Steve Nash retired after his body could no longer maintain the hard pace and keep up with the speed of the game. Eventually, Sid Crosby and Ben Zobrist will have to retire. Someday, you and I will as well.

Instead of citing some business article about the value of overcoming, let me ask a "versus" question: What is the value of changing which game we play vs. getting back into the game?

Most of us aren't putting our bodies and mental health at risk by working one more year, but this question *will* eventually come up for all of us.

How can I get back into the game?

When I say we should work through injuries, that doesn't mean returning to the game too soon and sustaining longer lasting damage. It *does* mean overcoming your injuries and obstacles to the degree you can manage, and at the pace you can maintain.

During the process of writing this book, my mother died in the hospital. 53 days later, my father died. I tried to honor my father's motto to "Keep on keeping on!" and I jumped back into the saddle too soon. Four days after my father died, I flew to a client's headquarters to kick off a project. Many things went wrong. Upon landing I went to the emergency room, key players at the client's headquarters became consumed with work emergencies of their own, and more. When the client learned of my father's recent passing, they encouraged me to go back home and that we could resume the project soon. I did, and we did. After having more time to grieve, I got back in the game and did so effectively.

Keep on Keeping on!

One day I decided to go for a walk, and about a third of a mile from home I had to sit down because I was sobbing. I called a friend who came over right away and sat with me. Later he gave me a ride home. Several other friends came, sat, and talked with me, sharing my grief.

With help from my wife, family, and friends, I was able to implement my father's motto, to "Keep on Keepin' On." It's a motto that had served me well in terms in the past while doing homework and other tasks. The truth is quite simple: often you just have sit down and do it (we all remember high school – somehow, despite all of our hopes and desires, our homework never got done all by itself).

Action Plan: Dealing with setbacks

Write down your biggest challenge or setback, then answer these corresponding questions:

- Can I solve this just by "Keep on Keeping on?"

- Why do I need/want to overcome this?

- What resources do I have to help me overcome this?

- Who can help me with advice, or even some of the heavy lifting?

- What problems will I encounter?

- How can I solve those problems (preferable in advance through preparation and preemptive action)?

Pictures

6 MVP Community Event, including Kathy Jacobs, Michael Washington, and Octavio Hernandez

7 Hal Hostetler, the author, Chris Price (MVP Lead), Rob Richardson

8 Author's MVP Trophy

9 10-year Microsoft MVP Ring

10 What if MVPs from the 4 sports had adjoining lockers? (Photo by David B Moore)

11 What the locker of a Microsoft MVP might look like (Photo by David B. Moore)

12 MVP Award Box

13 Thiago Oliveira & Andre Oliveira at MVP Summit wearing an inspiring message that captures the essence of a Microsoft MVP

14 Author holding his MVP Trophy in 2014

15 This is what an MVP looks like when he fakes his surprise the way the winners of pageants do

Part III How do MVPs help everyone else around them be better?

So many times, we see where the addition of an MVP caliber player transforms a team into a contender.

Steve Nash transformed the Phoenix Suns in the 2004-2005 season from 2nd to last place to 1st place. Dale Murphy came into his own in 1982 going from 13 home runs the previous year to 36 home runs that year and .247 Batting Average to .281, transforming the Braves from 5th place in their division to 1st place and advancing to the playoffs.

In Sid "the Kid" Crosby's 2nd year in the NHL he exploded for a league leading 120 points, winning the Hart Memorial Trophy (MVP) in the process and elevating his team from 5th in their division to 2nd.

In 1987 Steve Young's arrival transformed a team that was amazing with their great but fragile quarterback to a robust team able to win even when star quarterback, Joe Montana, was injured and on the sideline. In 1988 Young's performance replacing an injured Montana made the difference between making the playoffs and not. That year they went on to win the Super Bowl.

So how do MVPs elevate their teams into contenders?

- Chapter 5: Passing the Ball
- Chapter 6: Praise your teammates
- Chapter 7: Care about the game and others

Chapter 5: Passing the Ball

Pass, Pass, Pass (Steve Nash)

My Chance to Shine

Rob Richardson

Run or Pass (Steve Young)

More Assists Per Game (Sid the Kid Crosby)

Josep Solanes

Show and Go (Ben Zobrist)

Microsoft MVPs

Brian Desmond

Passing the Torch (Dale Murphy)

How Passing the ball increases business value

Action Plan: How can I pass the ball better and more often?

Pass, Pass, Pass (Steve Nash)

 With a trip to the 2005 Western Conference finals on the line, Steve Nash drove down the lane, drew in the Dallas Maverick defenders, and then made a great pass to Shawn Marion, just as he made an excellent cut and then sank a clutch basket to put the game out of reach (VintageDawkins, 2017).

All around, Steve Nash put up clutch numbers in that game, playing 50 minutes, scoring 39 points, 9 rebounds, and even earning 1 block. Most importantly, though, he dished up 12 assists. A dozen times in that game he helped his teammates shine in their moment of glory and as they led the team to victory (Phoenix Suns at Dallas Mavericks Box Score, May 20, 2005, n.d.).

This sort of behavior is contagious. Numerous times during this same game, teammate A'mare Stoudemire can be seen setting picks and screens to give Steve open looks for shooting three pointers and other jump shots. Unlike assists, they don't even track that as a stat. In that way, A'mare was being an MVP to Steve and making him even better!

What possessed Steve to pass so often?

Why would Steve Nash pass often? When did he learn this behavior and from whom? In Steve's own words, "My dad." His dad had played semi-pro soccer. "In the backyard or after games as a kid, ... He always appreciated the unselfish. He never said, 'Wow, three goals!' Instead he said, 'Brilliant vision to see your teammate coming in behind the play,' or, 'So unselfish to pass when you could've shot. That makes me proud.' I know that's not normal and I'm grateful" (Nash, 2015). What influence our fathers can have over us!

> "So unselfish to pass when you could've shot.
> That makes me proud."
> – A typical comment from Steve Nash's
> father to Steve during his childhood.

My Chance to Shine

In 2008 I was working very closely with Brad Turner, then a Microsoft MVP and now a Microsoft employee. Though I was already an MVP, in many ways Brad was a mentor to me, and he encouraged me to begin a blog. One day while working on an early Beta version of a Microsoft product (Microsoft Forefront Identity Manager 2010 also called FIM), Brad and I discovered how to turn on tracing which greatly improved our ability to understand what the product was doing and how to troubleshoot it. Brad encouraged me to write up our discovery and post it to my blog. (http://blog.ilmbestpractices.com/2008/11/under-hood-of-ilm-2-part-1-enable-wcf.html). Weeks later, Brad was communicating with Microsoft Tech Support trying to resolve an issue with the Beta product and they referred him to this blog article, telling him that many people found it helpful in their troubleshooting. He chuckled and told them that he was sitting next to me and assisted me in writing the article. For me it was a thrill that in the absence of full documentation, Microsoft was sending people to read my blog article.

As I have interviewed or spoken with other MVPs in my niche of Identity Management, one MVP has constantly been mentioned as a giver of opportunities to shine. His name is Gil Kirkpatrick. For most of the 2000's Gil was employed as the CTO of a company called NetPro. At Gil's encouragement, NetPro put on the Directory Experts Conference (later The Experts Conference) and continued to do so for ten or eleven years until it was cancelled after a few mergers (Quest bought NetPro and then Dell bought Quest). In his capacity as founder and content chair, Gil gave out speaking slots to over a hundred different people, many of whom were first time public speakers. Microsoft MVP's Joe Kaplan and Brian Desmond (both of whom I interviewed for this book) cite him as someone that passed them the ball and gave them a chance to shine.

Me, too.

Gil gave me my first chance to speak on Identity Management. In late 2006, less than a year after I had discovered Identity Management and decided that it was my life's work (at least for a while), I had taken a training class delivered by James Booth (then one of four MVP's worldwide for Identity Management). With a little encouragement from James, I submitted two papers to Gil Kirkpatrick, for the Directory Experts Conference of 2007. I asked James for a little endorsement to Gil to help my cause. When I found out I was chosen to speak, I was ecstatic! I would get to go to the conference for free and I would get to rub shoulders with MVP's like Brad Turner, James Booth, and Craig Martin, all three of whom I had looked up to since I discovered Identity Management!

In his capacity as founder and content
chair, Gil Kirkpatrick gave out speaking
slots to over a hundred different people,
many of whom were first time public speakers.

Speaking at the conference was for me like a rookie's first turn at bat in the Major Leagues, or throwing your first pass in a pro football game, or making an awesome assist in pro basketball or hockey. Unlike the pro athlete or entertainer, our loved ones don't often get to watch our performance during these exciting moments, but thanks to the kindness of Gil's coworker, Christine McDermott, I was able to get my father a pass to the conference and he was able to see me deliver my sessions. He reported that I appeared authoritative without being overbearing, and that I did an excellent job, speaking clearly and handling questions. Indeed, my performance in those talks had an impact on my becoming a Microsoft MVP. The memory of that conference in 2007 is especially poignant now that my father has passed. A little more than one year after the conference, I was renewed as a Microsoft MVP for the first time, and I had Microsoft send my father a recognition letter as well. My father promptly scanned it and sent out an email to all my siblings titled: "David and Bill Gates," saying "This is a significant accomplishment and a recognition by the technical community of Dave's work and abilities." I wasn't in competition with my siblings, but I was glad to receive my father's approval and praise.

Once more Gil Kirkpatrick has gotten into the conference game. In conjunction with Mickey Bresman of Semperis and his team, including MVP Darren Mar-Elia, he has cofounded the HIP Conference (Hybrid Identity Protection Conference), designed to foster the same level of community engagement that the Directory Experts Conference had created. I attended and spoke at the 2nd annual HIP Conference in November of 2018.

Rob Richardson
Gilbert, AZ USA

MVP 2014 - Present

Category: Visual Studio and

Development Technologies,

Previously: ASP.NET and IIS

Rob started out with the goal of acquiring the extensive knowledge required to become an MVP. He failed. However, his follow up was to start speaking frequently and leading Arizona's Southeast Valley .NET user group. Soon after, he was nominated and became an MVP.

Leading user groups to empower others, Rob asks himself, "Can I scale my knowledge to 8 or 10 others?" He also sees the "hive mind" as a way to resolve roadblocks that individual members experience. Under his twitter handle (Rob_Rich), he has spoken across the USA and abroad.

To give back, Rob co-led two hackathons called AZ Give Camp in 2017. The "prize" for these hackathons was to build software for a charity. He contributed to the Humanitarian Toolbox, built a scheduling app for smoke alarm installs, and makes significant open source contributions to Gulp (a toolkit for automating and streamlining web development).

Rob is driven by his passion to support his wife and two children.

RedGate Software asked Rob to speak in Austin, TX for his first non-local speech. He illustrated continuous integration with SQL Server databases (a daunting task) using the previous night's backup. This led to speaking in Seattle and then at Prairie Code and Dev Connections. He eventually co-authored a book on SQL Server Source Control.

Rob recalls two pivotal moments in his career. Once, he looked up and realized he had more degrees than everyone else and had specialized in a proprietary programming language unlikely to see significant growth. He needed to train himself in new areas. More recently, Rob had an epiphany about handling questions on stage, and began developing the ability to think on his feet. He now enjoys giving interactive presentations.

https://mvp.microsoft.com/en-us/PublicProfile/5000872
https://www.linkedin.com/in/erobrich/
https://twitter.com/rob_rich
Rob: David's Book Reviews, notes and videos on DavidPLundell.com

Run or Pass (Steve Young)

In basketball, when you have the ball you can attempt to score or pass, and we expect some of both, but in football we think – of course – that the Quarterback is supposed to pass the ball. However, it wasn't always that way in general, and it wasn't always this way for Steve. In fact, in high school Steve played mainly as a running quarterback. His great speed enabled him to outrun many defenders. In college, Steve began to learn how to be a drop back passer. He still ran for 18 touchdowns, but he passed for more than triple his number of rushing touchdowns, connecting with receivers for touchdowns 56 times. At one point then BYU QB coach Mike Holmgren scolded him about running so much, telling him, "Your receivers… will quit if you keep doing that. Stay in the pocket. Be patient" (Young S. &., 2016).

Steve learned this lesson, and eventually he teamed up with Jerry Rice to connect for more touchdown passes than any other duo in NFL history. Jerry Rice was already viewed as a great wide receiver when Steve Young became his teammate. In fact, Jerry Rice already had a great quarterback throwing to him, a guy named, Joe Montana, who connected with Rice for 67 touchdowns. Steve Young and Jerry Rice ultimately connected for 92 touchdowns, 10 more than any other combo until 2004 (Reevy, 2014).

More Assists Per Game (Sid the Kid Crosby)

In hockey, like in basketball, it seems that the glory is in scoring. However, a true team player knows that often you can best help your team by passing the puck to your teammate so that he can put it in the net. Sid "the Kid" Crosby is marvelous at scoring goals and assists. In his first year in the NHL, with the Pittsburgh Penguins, he broke the franchise rookie record for assists with 63 and over the course of his career he has led the whole league in "assists per game" three times: 2007-2008, 2012-2013, and 2013-2014. In fact, as of July 2018, Sid leads all active players with 0.82 assists per game (Hockey Reference, n.d.).

In one game, Crosby moved the puck down the ice against the Florida Panthers and was pushed into the corner when he did an amazing no look, left-handed, backwards pass to No 9 Pascal Dupuis, who put the puck in the net for a goal to help lead the team to victory. (https://www.youtube.com/watch?v=RYI0B94pqbk&t=89s).

Josep Solanes

Tarragona, Spain

MVP 2014 – 2015

Category: Windows Server for Small and Medium Businesses

Cloud and Datacenter Management

Josep "passes the ball" to his small and medium-sized business clients. He identified a need to make better use of technology, especially Microsoft technology and specifically in the Catalonia region of Spain. To this end, he created a blog in Catalan that offered numerous step-by-step tutorials solving common business problems encountered when using Office 365. Josep later added Spanish language versions of his tutorials in order to attract a wider audience and help more people.

Josep keeps his skills sharp by constantly playing a mental game as he reviews new technology, asking himself, "How can I use this to solve customers' problems?" This client-centered approach sets Josep apart and allows him to quickly identify areas of opportunity and improvement for his clients.

Josep's driving motivation is to improve his clients' systems and help them overcome the challenges that arise in their businesses.

When I interviewed Josep he had already been informed that he was not renewed for the MVP program. In fact, his badge designated him as an "MVP Alumnus," and he let me know that he was signing up for the MVP Reconnect program.

"Josep keeps his skills sharp by constantly playing a mental game as he reviews new technology, asking himself, 'How can I use this to solve customers' problems?'"

---

https://www.linkedin.com/in/jmsolanes/
https://twitter.com/jmsolanes
https://mvp.microsoft.com/en-us/PublicProfile/5001143
Josep: David's notes and videos on DavidPLundell.com

Show and Go (Ben Zobrist)

In contrast to football, hockey, and basketball, you don't pass the ball in baseball in an attempt to score, but rather to prevent the other team from scoring. The baseball example of passing the ball is more figurative than literal. As mentioned earlier in the book, Ben Zobrist and three of his baseball friends produce the entertaining and informative "The Show and Go Podcast" (https://theshowandgo.podbean.com/). Where they discuss "the mental side of baseball, the things that might help younger players," high school kids, and "younger minor leaguers that are just getting started in [professional] baseball." They really hope to help "the younger generation of players and parents and the coaches." They just got started in early 2018, and as of April 2018 they have three episodes available. The latest episode, in which they discuss "Player/Coach Communication," has great advice about giving and receiving of feedback. Advice that I would apply in business as well as baseball (Dillard, 2018).

As Ben and his friends share their knowledge and experience, they are passing the ball to the next generation of players, both in baseball and in life. Well done, gentlemen!

Microsoft MVPs

In my interviews with the Microsoft MVPs, I didn't want to ask them to boast; in fact, despite their blogging and high profiles, most are quite modest. Instead of asking them about the times they passed the ball, or how many assists they have recorded, I asked them about times the ball was passed to them. In the process I also learned about many times they passed the ball.

Gretchen (Opferkew) Mann has completed many successful passes and recorded many assists; serving on the board of an international online CRM user group, she has encouraged many people to speak. In hockey terms, she gives them open looks at the net! She glowingly recounted the joy when many people she encouraged to speak came back to her later, exclaiming, "I used to see you speak and now I am speaking!"

Rob Richardson also helps many people make layups as he is always looking to give new people a chance to speak at the East Valley .NET Users group in Phoenix, AZ. Additionally, through encouraging many to participate in hackathons he gives them a chance to display their talents for a good cause (helping out various charities).

Keeping with the metaphor, Jessica Moss caught a pass another co-worker had bobbled. The co-worker had invited her to co-present at an SQL Teach event in Canada. When he was suddenly unable to attend, Jessica had to present all by herself.

For Pablo Di Loreto, an acquaintance named Erica noticed his blogging and speaking, and told him of the MVP program. She encouraged him to focus his contributions, in order to provide more value to the community. His boss, Emiliano Estevez, Director at Algeiba, was also a Microsoft MVP, and encouraged him to use his valuable experience to lift others and help them to find the shortcuts.

I view Mike Halsey of the UK as an MVP among MVPs. During several of the MVP summits he has led sessions teaching MVPs how to make high quality videos. Talk about giving others a chance to shine!

Similarly, Kathy Jacobs was well ahead of the trend with social media and strongly encouraged the MVPs to take advantage of it, oftentimes teaching us how. Surprisingly, many of us who pride ourselves on being cutting edge resisted the move to social media. I attended her session and that is what got me reluctantly on board with using it.

Josep Solanes is always finding ways to pass the ball to his customers in Catalonia, Spain. He looks for solutions to their problems and writes step by step tutorials on how to solve common business problems using Office365. He publishes his articles in both Catalan and Spanish.

Andy Milford, of RDPSoft, stepped up to the plate and delivered big. Following a freemium model, he provides free and premium tools that replace and enhance the functionality lost when Microsoft pulled these utilities from Windows.

When he saw Microsoft remove some tools from Windows Server 2012 that had been used to administer remote connections to servers and remote desktop sessions, Andy Milford of RDPSoft stepped up to the plate and delivered big. Following a freemium model, he provides free and premium tools that replace and enhance the functionality lost when Microsoft pulled these utilities from Windows.

Brian Desmond

Chicago, IL, USA

MVP 2003 – Present

Category: Enterprise Mobility. Previously: Windows NT Domains, Directory Services

Brian Desmond holds a singular distinction by being the only MVP that I know of who earned his MVP recognition while he was still in high school. Although he is very confident in his knowledge and skills, Brian is also extremely modest about his beginnings in the MVP program. When discussing his trajectory from curious high school student to MVP, he humbly refers to his early activities as nothing more than answering questions in the newsgroups "back when that was a thing."

Brian has spoken at many conferences, among them the Directory Experts Conference, The Experts Conference, and Tech-Ed (now MS Ignite). He has also written two books. However, despite his success as a speaker and an author, his main passion – and contribution – continues to be answering questions on the forums.

Brian delivered a session at the recent MVP Summit 2018, where he shared with the other MVPs the lessons that he has learned in his business.

Brian keeps sharp learning as he shares, and reports that the MVP program has provided him a great network of friends from all over the world.

> "Brian...earned his MVP recognition while he was still in high school."

https://mvp.microsoft.com/en-us/PublicProfile/8596
https://twitter.com/brdesmond
https://www.linkedin.com/in/briandesmond/
David's Book Reviews, Notes and Videos on DavidPLundell.com

Passing the Torch (Dale Murphy)

It is common baseball wisdom that if you will be followed in the batting order by a great hitter, especially a power hitter, that you will get better pitches to hit, because they can't intentionally walk you if a runner is on second and first base is open without risking the next guy cleaning up with a home run.

Murphy usually batted third in the lineup, and while I would like to provide you an analysis that shows that the first two batters did significantly better when Dale was in the lineup than when he wasn't, I can't. You see, Dale had a streak of playing consecutive games, 740 consecutive games. So, there isn't much evidence during his peak years of what batting was like without him.

However, Dale passed the ball in a much more significant way. In 1990 he noticed that his beloved Atlanta Braves were struggling (as was he at the time). He also noticed that the Braves were rebuilding – adding a lot of young guys to the team, among them John Smoltz and Tom Glavine, two pitching talents who would later win the Cy Young award, given to the best pitcher in the league. He didn't want to put the team in the awkward position "of figuring out whether to renew his contract (even though his best years may well be behind him) or release him (usually against popular opinion.)," so Murph approached the general manager and told him that he "wanted the Braves to explore the possibility of getting something out of the situation, instead of [him] just leaving them as a free agent" (Murphy, Getting Traded to the Phillies - The Rest of the Story, 2011).

Dale asked to be traded to clear the way for the young guys and he wanted the team to still get some value out of it. I still remember in August of 1990 reading in the Contra Costa Times or watching on ESPN how the young player, David Justice, who took over for Murphy, felt. David said, "It is like taking over for God." The commentator (or writer), however, felt compelled to note that "God was batting in the .220's."

"It is like taking over for God."
– David Justice,
On taking Dale Murphy's spot in the outfield.

How Passing the ball increases business value

Brian Desmond was even passing the ball to other Microsoft MVPs, teaching them valuable tidbits he learned from his business. I mean really, who does this? Who shares such great tidbits with competitors? Honestly, over half of the people in the room were Brian's competitors. So why share? Because like most of us MVPs, we feel an intense desire to share knowledge and to help everyone else around us be better. The reality is that it won't hurt Brian's business at all. In fact, it will help it, because it establishes Brian as an expert even among other experts. He will receive referrals and he will be respected.

One Fortune 500 CIO I worked with passed the ball frequently to his subordinates by giving them a chance to grow, even going so far as to let them take over some of the things that he loved doing.

Well-functioning teams are critical to business success. Patrick M Lencioni and many others have written reams of best sellers about how to create high performing teams.

In the world of computer programming, methodologies have been created (such as Agile) to try and get teams to work better together in producing high quality software quickly and at lower cost.

Action Plan: How can I pass the ball better and more often?

Most of us don't have someone at the scorer's table tracking the number of times we set up a teammate up for success. So we need to ask:

- Who can I involve in this project?
- Who can I collaborate with on this task?
- Who should I have lead this project?

Not sure how to pass the ball well? Situational Leadership II, from the Ken Blanchard Institute, explains how we should remember that people have different abilities for different tasks:

- A beginner may need to be managed closely – almost micro-managed (my term not theirs).
- A slightly more experienced person, who has learned how hard a task is, will need close supervision but also needs to be part of the decision-making process.
- Someone who can do the work but isn't yet confident about it needs a sounding board.
- Someone who is fully capable and confident just needs it delegated to them with clear expectations.

After a while some employees may get suspicious and think they are being setup to fail. Avoid this by having earnest conversations with them.

Chapter 6: Praise your teammates

This is our star catcher (Ben Zobrist)

As I interviewed Ben Zobrist at the airport, I met his two travelling companions: Nick, the trainer who was recently promoted to the majors after years of great work in the minors, and another gentleman. Not wanting to make assumptions, I asked, "Are you also with the team?" Ben's reaction was great. "This is our star catcher right here, Wilson Contreras." Wilson, from Venezuela, was just starting his second year. He had a pretty good rookie season, and Ben's praise will only bolster Wilson's confidence.

Joe Kaplan

Chicago, IL, USA

MVP 2003 – Present

Category: Enterprise Mobility + Security

Previously: Directory Services

Joe has been a repeat MVP for a very long time. He made his initial mark in the industry by answering questions about LDAP programming using the old NNTP (Newsgroups) forums. His follow-up was to write a book about LDAP programming. This work, <u>The .Net Developer's Guide to Directory Services Programming</u>, is a great reference book and currently features prominently on my bookshelf.

You can find Joe speaking at conferences, writing blogs, and working directly with product groups.

One of Joe's first opportunities to shine came from Gil Kirkpatrick (another MVP), who provided Joe with several chances to speak at the Directory Experts Conference and, later, The Experts Conference.

Meeting the business needs of his employer drives Joe to seek out new technology and allows him the opportunity to stay fresh and informed and to constantly improve.

Joe's greatest contributions outside the technical arena stem from his three children (future taxpayers!), and usually involve volunteering to help with things they love (sports, theater, etc).

https://www.linkedin.com/in/joe-kaplan-59bb761/
https://mvp.microsoft.com/en-us/PublicProfile/8673
Joe: David's Book Reviews, notes and videos on DavidPLundell.com

Young Credits Teammates

 Steve Young transitioned from a wishbone quarterback who had never been coached on how to do a three step drop into a drop back passer. While filling in for the great Jim McMahon, he also found a "great mentor" in Jim, who "taught him all sorts of things about throwing a football… but [the most important lesson] was confidence." During one game, McMahon got hurt and Young stepped in to throw a pair of touchdown passes that helped to seal the victory over the surging Colorado Buffaloes. Afterwards, Jim encouragingly told Steve, "I knew you could do it kid" (Young S. &., 2016).

Steve Young, NFL Hall of Fame Quarterback for the San Francisco 49ers, had just won the Super Bowl. How does he celebrate? By thanking those who have helped him, linemen and receivers. "[Bart] Oates…Steve Wallace, Jesse Sapolu, … Harris Barton … Brent Jones, Jerry Rice, and John Taylor ... I love these men" (Young S. , QB: My Life Behind the Spiral, 2016).

Reflecting on his Super Bowl win, Steve Young credited the coaches and teammates all around him, noting that he had a "tremendous opportunity," having been "taught by one of the greatest coaches of all time," presumably Bill Walsh, "one of the greatest players of all time," definitely Joe Montana, and "by a series of players that are going to" be in the Hall of Fame." Reflecting on this history, he observed that "[I was] getting trained to be great; now go see how good [I] can get" (NFL, 2016). I am amazed at the graciousness in how Steve refers to "one of the greatest players of all time" – Joe Montana, the man whose long shadow put a lot of pressure on Steve, and perhaps wasted some of his best years.

Most Gracious Man on the Planet

I was first nominated as a Microsoft MVP by Brad Turner. At the time there were only four Identity Management Microsoft MVPs in the whole world. In April of 2007, Brad nominated three people (all working for competitors) to become Microsoft MVPs.

Brad and I had become acquainted in the Microsoft Online forums for Identity Management and then over a lunch. As it turned out he and I lived only a 10-min drive apart. I confess I had a bit of a competitive streak and I loved to see my name rise above his on the top answerers scoreboard. While Brad has his competitive fires, he is more driven by a desire to lift others and graciously share credit.

Just before we were both scheduled to speak at a conference he indicated that he was having issues with a SQL query he was trying to write. Since that is one of my strengths, I invited him to drive over to my office and see if I couldn't help him.

Sure enough, I got his Recursive Common Table expression query (don't worry, that was some technical jargon) working so that he could have a report showing the hierarchy of people in a directory, from the CEO down to the non-managers. The next week during his talk he gave a big shout out of thanks to me in front of several hundred people and encouraged them to go see my sessions, even though I had just joined his chief competitor.

It was after this conference that Brad nominated me and two other competitors to be MVPs. All three of us received the award that July.

Brad became an MVP in my life, both by his example of graciousness and by helping me become an MVP, not to mention the help that his Identity Chaos blog was to me as I was learning Identity Management.

Additional Thanks

I would also be remiss if I didn't mention a few other individuals that had direct and indirect impacts on my Identity Management career. Back in the early 2000's, Hugh Simpson-Wells and James Cowling had written an excellent course on Microsoft's Identity Management product (MIIS, now known as MIM). It was so well written that when I discovered this field and product, I was able to use my access to the course as a Microsoft Certified Trainer, to build myself a rock-solid foundation in the product and the confidence to go implement it and teach it. When I wanted to learn more, I went for an advanced training class (also written by Simpson-Wells and Cowling) taught by a then Microsoft MVP named James Booth. A few months later I was honored to be hired by them and to work with these highly intelligent people.

Could Solomon have shared the credit any better (Sid the Kid Crosby)?

Early in his fourth NHL season, Sid "the Kid" Crosby made three assists and scored one goal to surpass the 100 goals, 200 assists, and 300 points benchmarks for his career. By passing Crosby the puck, his teammate Evgeni Malkin earned an assist recording the 200th point (goals plus assists) of his own career. Normally, when a player hits a milestone they get to keep that puck. But, in this instance two teammates hit big career milestones on the same play. Who got the puck? What did Sid "the Kid" do? He "asked the Penguins' equipment staff to split the puck and present half to Malkin" (Rossi, 2008).

Sid "the Kid" "asked the Penguins'
equipment staff to split the puck
and present half to [his teammate].

Nash names "names"

Scott Gradin, a volunteer assistant coach at Santa Clara University noted that "Even in high school [Nash] could have been far and away The Guy, The Star. But he shared the spotlight with his teammates." Noting, that such "selflessness and humility was a unique characteristic, especially for an eighteen-year-old" (Feschuk, 2014).

Nash credits Danny Ainge, his coach during his rookie year, with giving him "a huge vote of confidence," and Michael Finley with giving up the glory of being an All-Star in order to better lead their Dallas Mavericks team from last place to the Conference Finals, noting "how rare that unselfishness is in our game" and calling Finley "a true friend and teammate." It seems, that Steve truly treasured the time he had with Dirk Nowitzki when they "were nobodies … and … [would love to] play a few more games of HORSE and one-on-one." While Nash laments never having won the NBA championship, when the 2011 Nash-less Mavericks, led by his great friend Dirk, won "their championship … [he] couldn't be happier for them" (Nash, 2015).

When Nash won his first MVP award, he instantly shared the credit: "I definitely won this award because of my role on the team." He further downplayed his own abilities and gifts, "I didn't win this because I overpower people or I'm dominating people with physical ability, whether it's jumping or strength or height" (Bailey, 2007).

> "I definitely won this award because of my role on the team. I didn't win this because I overpower people or I'm dominating people with physical ability, whether it's jumping or strength or height."
> -Steve Nash, after winning his first
> MVP Award (Bailey, 2007)

As he retired, he credited Phoenix Suns teammate A'mare Stoudemire and his "big hands [and] quick feet" for making him "look like an artist at times." He also cited how the Phoenix Suns "Training Room Mafia … kept [him] on the court and … sane" (Nash, 2015). Given his back problems, the training room definitely deserves the credit that Nash dished out.

"What comes to mind are all the great teammates I've played with and the friends I've made through the years. Guys like Al Whitley, Chris Isherwood, Jason Sedlock, Drew Zurek, Rowan Barrett, Andrew Mavis, Rex Chapman, Leandro Barbosa, Raja Bell, Grant Hill and Rob Sacre. Nothing beats the times we've had through the years and that's what I'll remember most" (Nash, 2015).

Andy Milford

Atlanta, GA, USA

MVP 2016 – Present

Category: Enterprise Mobility (Specialty: Remote Desktop)

Andy is a Serial Entrepreneur who sold Dorian Software to IpSwitch in 2009 and founded RDPSoft in 2013. He seized his opportunity to shine in technology at Ogelthorpe University in Atlanta. In addition to earning several scholarships, he was unofficially mentored by Jenny Tomlinson, who identified practical and academic opportunities for him. As a sophomore, Andy started "messing around" with Windows NT, learned Windows 2000, and wrote tools to help manage Windows 2000.

Immensely grateful to Ogelthorpe University, Andy gives back through various philanthropic efforts, endowed the Carlisle Arts Enrichment Fund (http://bit.ly/AM-Carlisle), served on the board of trustees in 2008 as a young alumni representative (http://bit.ly/AM-Oglethorpe), and participated in a Singers 2017 Reunion show (http://bit.ly/AM-Singers).

Taking nothing for granted, Andy constantly picks the brains of really smart people, such as other MVPs, in order to stay sharp.

Andy became a Microsoft MVP via his tools and blog articles. While speaking at industry events, a Microsoft Product Group Manager took notice and nominated him to be a Microsoft MVP.

Serial Entrepreneur

In the interview Andy and I agreed that being a serial entrepreneur is better than being a lot of other "serial" types.

https://mvp.microsoft.com/en-us/PublicProfile/5001724
https://www.linkedin.com/in/andy-milford-3b658229/
https://twitter.com/RDPSoft
Andy: David's Notes and Videos on DavidPLundell.com

Owe the Award to My Teammates (Dale Murphy)

 Steve Wulf of Sports Illustrated quoted Dale Murphy as saying, "I really owe the award to my teammates. If we hadn't won the division, I wouldn't have won the award" (Wulf, 1983).

When long-time Atlanta Braves Manager (and sometime general manager) Bobby Cox retired in 2010, Dale Murphy wrote him, saying, "thank you for having confidence and patience with in me early in my career… the move to the outfield was only one way you changed the course of my life. There are hundreds of other ways—too many to name here–that you've made me a better player, a better teammate, and a better man" (Murphy, Thank you Bobby Cox!, 2011).

Microsoft MVPs

Andy Milford caught multiple great passes early in his career from several people at Ogelthorpe University in Atlanta (his alma mater), including his first manager for his job there, Jenny Tomlinson. Before his senior year he had the chance to mess around with computers and learn Windows NT and Windows 2000. On the job, with encouragement, he wrote tools to help manage the windows computers. Those efforts got him started on his career – a successful one in which he has built up two successful companies.

Joe Kaplan specifically recognized the aforementioned MVP Gil Kirkpatrick with giving him a great chance to shine by awarding him speaking slots at the Directory Experts Conference.

Business Value

In Dave Zielinski's article "Why Social Recognition Matters," he summarizes the efforts of various organizations to use social recognition, saying that it "capitalizes on employees' behavioral habits and new social technologies to give more people a voice in saying 'thanks'" (Zielinski, 2015).

In his seminal series of books on The Five Love Languages, Gary Chapman explains that each person has a primary and secondary love language:

- Gifts
- Quality Time
- Words of Affirmation
- Acts of Service
- Physical Touch

I believe that these apply as well to helping an employee feel appreciated and hence engaged. After I wrote the preceding, I discovered that Gary Chapman (with co-author Paul White) wrote a later book called The 5 Languages of Appreciation in the Workplace (Chapman & White, 2012). Indeed, these concepts are validated in part by Rod Wagner and James K Harter's well researched book 12 Elements of Great Managing, where they explain that one of the 12 keys to employee engagement is that "Someone at Work Cares about Me as a Person," and other elements illustrate how to get there (Wagner & Harter, 2014).

Wagner and Harter's "Recognition and praise" element corresponds to Chapman and White's "Words of Affirmation" and "Gifts." The Love or Appreciation Language of Quality time is touched on by three of the Elements of Great Managing: "Someone at Work Encourages My Development," "My Opinions Seem to Count," and "Talking About Progress."

The element of having "A Best Friend at Work" will typically involve some amount of physical touch, from handshakes to high fives to fist bumps to hugs. Of course, this is an area for caution, as there are some people that don't like hand shaking, let alone hugging. We never want to violate someone else's physical comfort zone; instead we want to understand others and approach them appropriately.

Action Plan: How can I praise my teammates?

First, observe what love or appreciation language matters most to those around you. Since most people will use their own primary language most often when appreciating others, you can observe how they show that appreciation. You could even informally survey people, asking in general if the company needs to offer more praise, gifts, or high fives in front of the group for a job well done, etc.

Set a calendar reminder in Outlook to use your company's employee social recognition system. If they don't have one, then send the person and their team an email with praise. Store these emails in a separate folder. Periodically review these to figure out how to show appreciation.

As part of your effort to be sincere, try to find ways to use their primary language of appreciation.

- Gifts
    - Use your corporate system or your own wallet to get a small thoughtful gift following your organization's policies.
    - People whose language is Gifts appreciate gift cards, but they appreciate even more the thought and effort the giver puts into choosing a personalized gift.
        - My wife tells me that every time she puts on a necklace that I purchased for her while I was on a business trip, she thinks, "Oh my husband bought this for me."
- Quality Time
    - Invite them to lunch or to accompany you to a conference or a meeting with higher ups.
    - Truly listen to their aspirations and worries.
- Acts of Service
    - Arrange coverage for them when on vacation.
    - Help them to take time off to see a loved one's play or sporting event.

- o At a meeting, serve the beverage or refreshment.
- Words of Affirmation
  - o When preparing for a presentation or speech, review the emails you stored and be sure to include shout outs to those that helped.
  - o In One on One settings, offer appropriate praise.
- Physical Touch
  - o When thanking them publicly, call them down to the front and offer a handshake, a high five or a fist bump.

Often you will combine multiple forms such as shaking hands while offering words of affirmation while also giving them a gift. Since praise is such a key motivator, it is critical that you do so effectively.

How to give praise?

- Be Sincere
  - o Don't offer praise for something you don't like.
    - ▪ You may not care for the overall performance of something but find a specific thing you genuinely like.
  - o No one likes insincere and/or vague praise.
  - o Don't offer backhanded praise mixed with criticism.
    - ▪ There are other times for constructive feedback.
- Be Specific
  - o Look for the specific good and explain why it is good.
  - o Specificity helps people know that you mean it.
  - o When you encourage behavior that you like, you will get more of it.
- Be Swift
  - o Give praise before you forget.
  - o Praising a behavior promptly will help reinforce the good behavior.

Right after a speech given by a friend or teammate, you could say or email, "I really like the story you shared in your speech about how Brad offered praise in his conference session. It helped me realize that I need to change the way I give praise." Even if you didn't like the overall speech or thought the delivery was boring, the next time this person speaks they will take time to seek out interesting stories, and perhaps next time it will be a little less boring.

Chapter 7: Care about the game and others

Forever Young

Nash Humanitarian MVP

Michael Washington

Sid "the Kid" Crosby helps the kids

Enter a warzone, anyone? Some Microsoft MVPs did!

Microsoft MVPs

MVPs of Autism

Naseem Tuffaha

Blood, Sweat and Tears

Jason Brimhall

Ben Zobrist – Committed Christian

Dale Murphy – Sportsman of the Year and Humanitarian Hall of Famer

Business value of giving back

Action Plan: How can I give back?

Almost without exception the Microsoft and Sports MVPs highlighted in this book give of themselves within their professional specialties as well as outside of it. In almost every case, their giving began before their successes. In fact, their successes frequently just gave them more leverage to increase their outside contributions of time and money.

Forever Young

In 1990, I had the chance to hear Steve Young speak. A young boy in our congregation was seriously ill, and someone acquainted with Steve invited him to visit the young boy, which morphed into him speaking to the youth of our congregation.

Three years later in 1993, Steve Young founded the Forever Young Foundation to pass on hope and resources in the aid of "the development, strength, and education of children." Steve and his wife Barb are co-chairs of the board, with Sterling Tanner as Executive Director, and the organization has several areas of focus (Forever Young

Foundation, n.d.). Full disclosure: Sterling is a distant cousin of mine and we used to be in the same congregation at church when I was a teenager.

8 to 80 Zones

Steve Young and Jerry Rice succeeded in finding the end zone together, connecting on 92 touchdown passes, 10 more than the next best quarterback and receiver combo, which was an NFL record until 2004 (Reevy, 2014). Off the field they didn't "find" a zone so much as "create" zones. Together they created the "8 to 80 Zones," so-called because Steve wore #8 and Jerry Rice #80, "which provide youth living in underserved communities the skills to pursue careers in technology and media." So far they have five locations: one near San Francisco, CA; another near Phoenix, AZ; one in Los Angeles; one in Hawaii; and another mobile one in Hawaii (Forever Young Foundation, n.d.).

Forever Young Zones

The foundation has two other kinds of Forever Young Zones: three Hospital Forever Young Zones and four Forever Young Media Zones.

The Hospital Zones give "seriously ill children" the tools for "exercising their imagination" in a "safe place" where they can "build supportive relationships" with the staff members that help them. Overall it gives the kids a place to take a break from their "serious illness and rigorous treatments" to "just be a child." They currently have three: one in Salt Lake City, UT; one near San Francisco, CA; and another near Phoenix, AZ (Forever Young Foundation, n.d.).

The Forever Young Media Zones "provide a state-of-the-art radio, TV, film and design studio, as well as a professional-quality recording studio with an isolated vocal booth and digital audio mixing," in hopes of enabling adolescents to gain hands on communications skills. According to the website they have four of these: two in Utah, one in Massachusetts, and one in Connecticut. They also have six partnerships with NFL Youth Education Towns (Forever Young Foundation, n.d.).

Sophie's Place

Starting in 2013 they also built four music therapy spaces in Children's hospitals called Sophie's Place and have two more in the design stage (Smith, 2017).

Engage Now Africa

The Forever Young foundation also focuses on helping Children in Africa by partnering with Engage Now Africa, an NGO (Non-Governmental Organization). They fund "schools, micro credit loans and humanitarian assistance" in order to "fight poverty, illiteracy, and disease" in "Ethiopia, Ghana, Sierra Leone, and Namibia." (Forever Young Foundation, n.d.)

Supporting Other Non-Profits

Finally, they support other nonprofits through GIVE Conferences, grants and weeklong training sessions to other nonprofits called Forever Young Institute.

Impacts

One mother of twins wrote about the impact the foundation had on her life and the short lives of her twin sons, calling the people of the foundation her "living angels." The foundation got her and her twin sons to Stanford University Hospital, "let [them] stay in [Steve's] home," and got them "experienced help to educate them on how to care" for the twins and even gave them a few hours to go on a date with her husband, something that had been missing from their lives (Suzzane61, 2014).

The Forever Young organization spends almost 95% of its three to four million dollars in annual donations on actual programs and receives four stars from Charity Navigator.

Nash Humanitarian MVP

Even more important than Steve Nash's astonishing clutch performance in 2005 to help lead his team to victory in Game 6 over the Dallas Mavericks, he helps others shine off the court with his charity work.

In 2015 I discovered that The Steve Nash Foundation (founded in 2001) had teamed up with Prizeo for a campaign to raise money in support of their mission to "increase access to critical resources for children in underserved communities." They had set up various levels of donations with various prizes, including chances to win a trip to New York City to watch or even play in a soccer match with Steve Nash. Yes, we all know that he's famous for basketball, but he grew up playing soccer, so I guess you could say it is his first love. I couldn't help myself; I had to donate $200, the MVP Level, to get my Steve Nash autographed T-Shirt and personalized signed photo.

Steve Nash's foundation also has a several areas of focus.

BC Grants

"Since 2006, the Foundation's [British Columbia, Canada] Grants program has delivered over $900,000 back into [the] community" with grants to "direct health and education services to underserved children." (Steve Nash Foundation, n.d.)

Paraguay

Steve's foundation also carries out many projects in Paraguay (the homeland of his now ex-wife), including a "post-operative pediatric cardiology ward" providing infants and children a safe place to recover after heart surgery. Steve and his foundation also lent a big hand to build a center to help with critical women's health issues through preventative care and education, seeing thousands of patients in its first year of operation.

Educare

Through his Educare efforts, his foundation has contributed over $2 million to establish a national network of high quality early learning centers for low income families. There is "nothing more powerful than watching a child have access to high quality learning opportunities." (Steve Nash Foundation, n.d.)

Reach

The Steve Nash Foundation has also setup a Reach program to help kids learn Agility, Balance, Coordination and Speed and to keep them active throughout their life. This program is designed to be incorporated into PE programs, and after school clubs like Boys and Girls clubs. (Steve Nash Foundation, n.d.)

The Starting Five

Finally, The Starting Five (Steve Nash Foundation, n.d.) focuses on enhancing childhood development in the first five years by helping encourage Dads to be a bit more involved and teaching Mom and Dad to do the three T's:

- Tune In More
- Talk More
- Take Turns

In keeping with the gracious spirit of MVP's, Nash credits the way "Jenny Miller has run my foundation for over 10 years, and she has never once left me or our mission exposed along the way. We're childhood friends and her immense talent matches the trust I have in her" (Nash, 2015).

Michael Washington

Pasadena, CA, USA

MVP 2007 – 2018

Category: Visual Studio and

Development Technologies

Michael writes books, maintains blogs, and speaks at conferences like Visual Studio Live! Michael loves the passionate and inspiring conversations that take place among the attendees after the talks at these conferences.

Michael is not satisfied to merely contribute to the community; when a group lacks a home, he will host it. In early 2011, enthusiasts of LightSwitch (at the time a new technology from Microsoft for web developers) didn't have a place to submit questions, ask for help, or offer assistance to others. When Michael became aware of this, he created and hosted an online forum for LightSwitch users until Microsoft eventually set up their own.

Michael uses his technical skills to help a hospital in St. Louis analyze patient outcomes, trying to determine if someone is suffering from sepsis; an accurate assessment is critical to combat this terrible killer in hospitals.

> Michael uses his technical skills to help a hospital in St. Louis analyze patient outcomes, trying to determine if someone is suffering from sepsis; an accurate assessment is critical to combat this terrible killer in hospitals.

Michael is now focusing on Cognitive Services (machine learning/artificial intelligence), and authored a book titled <u>Microsoft Azure Machine Learning Studio (for the Non-Data Scientist)</u> in the style of the "Complete Idiot's Guide" or "For Dummies" books. This is in addition to his eight previously published books on web development.

https://mvp.microsoft.com/en-us/PublicProfile/38654
https://www.linkedin.com/in/michael-a-washington/
David's Book Reviews, Notes and Videos on DavidPLundell.com

Sid "the Kid" Crosby helps the kids

 Sid "the Kid" Crosby received a $20,000 bonus for being part of the gold medal hockey team at the 2010 Vancouver Olympics, which he promptly donated to the <u>Sydney Crosby Foundation</u>, founded in 2009 (Canadian Press, 2010).

Teen Lounge at IWK Health Center

Sydney used his foundation to help develop a "teen lounge for patients at the IWK Health Center … near his hometown [in Nova Scotia]," that gives these patients a safe place to enjoy some of the typical social experiences that kids their age who aren't hospitalized get to enjoy (Staff Writer/Pittsburgh Penguins, 2011).

"We are thrilled with Sidney's support of the IWK and Child Life program," said Brad Jacobs, vice president of development for the IWK Foundation. "Through this project and the Stanley Cup visit two summers ago, he has been a real Champion for the Maritimes patients and families we serve" (Staff Writer/Pittsburgh Penguins, 2011). Of course he says "Champion," but I hear, "MVP."

This teen lounge sounds similar in concept to Steve Young's Hospital Forever Young Zones. Good on both of them!

As the father of three dyslexic boys, one of whom has Autism, and another who had a severe birth defect that led to two hospitalizations (right after birth for two weeks and at age six for a week), reading about this kindness brought tears to my eyes.

Other Charity Work

"He has done charity work with multiple charities such as: Make-A-Wish; Big Brothers Big Sisters; the Boys & Girls Club; Special Olympics of Allegheny County; The Bone Marrow Transplant/Oncology Unit of UPMC Shadyside; The DePaul School for Hearing and Speech; and many others to add to the already admirable list" (Marin, 2011).

Got Started Early

According to his Junior High Vice Principal, Sid has always had an interest in helping those with special needs and is "an amazing role model who was really kind to students in the learning centre and to special needs kids" (Sidney Crosby, n.d.).

Mark Messier Leadership Award

The NHL has also recognized Sidney's efforts, awarding him the Mark Messier Leadership award in Jan 2010. The award is given "to the player who exemplifies great leadership qualities to his team, on and off the ice during the regular season" (NHL.com, 2018).

Enter a warzone, anyone? Some Microsoft MVPs did!

Years before rising through the ranks at Microsoft to become a Sr. Director and manage the MVP program, Naseem Tuffaha worked in the field for Microsoft in the Middle East and Africa, where he worked closely with many MVPs and became really good friends with several of them. One experience he recounted, though, really shined forth with the MVP spirit.

A community of young people in the Gaza strip had formed Dot Net programmers' clubs and were really eager to host Microsoft training and events to further their development skills. They also wanted the morale boost of knowing that big companies were paying attention to them, even in their little corner of the world. A group of MVPs from Jordan volunteered to go. In theory, you could drive from Jordan to the Gaza Strip, but that isn't advisable. At the time the personal security situation was very tense because of the conflicts in the region, and Microsoft's security personnel even advised that they couldn't guarantee the safety of Microsoft personnel, and needed to be sure that they were aware of the risk. "But the MVP's never hesitated for an instant." They only reported one airstrike during their stay.

> "But the MVP's never hesitated for an instant."
> – Nassem Tuffaha

While serving a mission for my church, I was in a few spots where gunfire could be heard and even saw some guns drawn in anger (and fortunately not fired), but volunteering to going into an area that was under threat of active bombardment is something quite different.

Microsoft MVPs

United Way to Meals on Wheels

University of Virginia alum Jessica Moss gives back by serving the community with her Alumni group, repainting school walls, helping United Way, and providing food through Meals on Wheels.

Non-profit

Gretchen (Opferkew) Mann started her career in the non-profit world and lived in Africa, working to improve the quality of life for many people. Upon returning to the United States, she sought a degree in counseling and then non-profit management, all with the aim of helping others. After ten years and seven schools she graduated, but discovered that along the way that she was already helping people and making the world a better place by using her technology skills.

Helping others' voices be heard

Hal Hostetler of Tucson is the consummate volunteer, lending his specialized expertise in TV and Radio to several causes. Hal is a key volunteer for helping Cactus Intertie maintain their two-way radio base stations, and in doing so maintains "wide area emergency communications coverage, supports various public service events and provides training to the general public where applicable" (www.intertie.org). Hal also supports a religious radio station in Tucson, Arizona. Most notably, Hal (CPBE, WA7BGX) serves as Net Control for and runs the monthly chapter meeting of HF HAMNet on the second Sunday of every month at 2400 GMT on frequency 14.205MHz. This chapter was created to help HAM Radio operators who aren't close to a local chapter advance their technical skills, develop comradery, and be prepared to serve as vital communications links in emergencies (www.sbe.org/sections/hamnet.php).

Saving lives

Sepsis, according to Wikipedia, afflicts one million Americans annually and has a 30% chance of death. Michael Washington employed his machine learning skills to help develop a system wherein a St. Louis hospital could more accurately determine if patients have sepsis. This was accomplished by mining the data in the electronic health records (EHR).

Parle vous Olympics?

In the 2002 Winter Olympics, Jason Brimhall volunteered as an official French language Translator. Jason helps local schools with their technical needs and spends time mentoring struggling readers. Additionally, Brimhall has been involved in Boy Scouts of America for 30 years, currently serving as a Cub Scout Den leader. He also coaches little league basketball, football, and baseball.

Serial Volunteer

With the "word sucker stamped on [her] forehead" and "serial volunteer" stamped on her business card, former Microsoft MVP Kathy Jacobs is always looking to help. She and her husband for four years volunteered their sound and lighting expertise in benefit of a community theater in Rochester, NY. Later, she and her husband volunteered as Brownie leaders. Kathy has also served with the Association of Personal Computer User Groups (an international group supporting user groups in USA, Canada and Australia). Why? Simply put, she "can't imagine not doing it."

MVPs of Autism

One former MVP has founded a company that seeks out about 75% of their employees from among people on the Autism Spectrum. He spends time educating others (including MVPs) about his perspectives on Autism. He once mentioned how the defense apparatus of one country that is surrounded by enemies has employed people on the spectrum to help them find patterns to detect threats to their homeland – threats they otherwise would have missed. Is this former MVP sacrificing profits or is he seeing an underutilized resource and figuring out how to help them make great contributions?

On that note, I can't help but mention that in our local community a number of people are MVPs to many autistic children and their parents and have given countless hours to commiserate and counsel with beleaguered parents as well as seeking to change local laws to assist these families. One such woman, Cynthia McCluskey, just announced her retirement after 17 years in this effort and a battle with cancer. People like Cynthia truly express the spirit of the MVP.

Naseem Tuffaha

Redmond, WA, USA

Sr. Director at Microsoft

As a Microsoft employee, Naseem is not eligible for the MVP Program. However, he expresses all of the traits of a true MVP. At the time of my interview with Naseem, his organization was in charge of the MVP program and had been for two years (this has since changed). Naseem started in the field in the Middle East and Africa with much smaller teams. In these smaller and developing markets, the connection to – and dependence on – MVPs is much higher, as these MVPs led events for Naseem and gave valuable feedback.

Naseem also makes sure to give back. In one instance, he and some MVPs from Jordan went into the war-torn Gaza Strip to teach local youngsters coding skills and give them a glimpse of a better future.

According to Naseem, the MVP program doesn't have an ROI goal, but it points back to Microsoft's core mission to empower every individual and corporation to achieve more.

Naseem's favorite thing about the MVP program is the idea that you can make a difference beyond yourself. This is a core value that underpins a successful community. It is about people choosing to come together. With a firm belief that people can grow, and that you can play a role in how people develop, you can strengthen communities. In the process of making others better, you make yourself better. When you enter a situation with the expectation to give and not receive, everyone gives and everyone receives.

Naseem has worked with a medical relief organization helping thousands of children by bringing them to the US for treatment, as well as bringing doctors and equipment to them. He is also working to build a pediatric cancer center in a remote and otherwise underserved region.

> "Naseem has worked with a medical relief organization helping thousands of children by bringing them to the US for treatment, as well as bringing doctors and equipment to them."

---

https://www.linkedin.com/in/naseemtuffaha/
Naseem: David's Notes and Videos on DavidPLundell.com

Blood, Sweat and Tears

After talking about various accomplishments of mine, I suppose it is too late to plead modesty, and if I didn't discuss my own "off the court" contributions, it would leave many readers wondering whether I practice these things, too. I do; nothing quite as dramatic as entering a war zone, but I do donate blood – my goal is a power red donation twice a year.

My community service revolves around my family, my neighborhood, Boy Scouts of America, and Church.

Need a job?

Amid the Great Recession that started in 2008, I was asked at church to serve as an Employment Specialist and help people who are out of work or need to upgrade their employment. Several times a month, I manned an employment center where I would meet with people who showed up needing help. Using an excellent manual written by another man who had served in the same position, I and six others would assess the job seeking skills of these individuals, listen to their goals, and help them refine their skills. We often started with resume writing and would progress to networking skills and finally interviewing skills. It was a great feeling to see someone enter with apprehension about their future and leave with faith and hope; those who later reported back that they had found new employment made the feeling that much more powerful.

One time was initially quite frustrating for me, as a woman needed a change but didn't have a clear goal – "something in the service industry." *Wow, that's too broad, we need to refine that*, I told her. She promised that she would. A week later, an elderly woman called me. She and her husband ran a large business and had donated hundreds of millions of dollars to various causes (including two different universities), and she was looking for a new personal assistant. The instant she described what she needed, my mind turned to the woman without a clear goal. I made the connection between the two of them and she proceeded to work for her for several years, during which time I always got invited to their Christmas parties.

Who do you think you are?

Church has also provided many opportunities to serve, all volunteer and unpaid. I have taught young kids, teenagers, and adults. I have also served in three different Elders quorum presidencies (think a men's outreach ministry that assigns each man to visit between 1-4 other families to look after them). One of my more interesting roles has been helping others with family history/genealogy.

I once invited the CEO of the company where I was working at the time to get together, offering to help him learn more about his family history. We had a great time, and he learned how his paternal grandfather come over from Europe as a two-old boy, something he hadn't known because his own father had passed away when he was quite young.

After a while, I was asked to lead the volunteer efforts of a couple of thousand members of the church in doing indexing. The objective is to make more records accessible to searching by viewing images of birth certificates, draft cards, ship passenger manifests, marriage certificates, and death certificates, and typing the data from key fields. In this way, people can search for their relatives and ancestors and learn more about where they came from.

I took on this role in the middle of 2011. The year prior, fewer than 60 out of 2000+ possible people had participated, and they had processed about 250,000 records. In 2011, we had just under 100 participate and processed nearly 300,000 records. Heading into 2012 we faced a challenge. Because of a combination of families moving and a realignment of some of the congregations, we had lost the people who had completed over 1/3 of the record inputs (110,000). Despite this setback, and with careful thought and consideration, I felt that a goal of 450,000 was achievable. I then set out a plan of how to get there: visiting the leaders of the various congregations, with their permission visiting the congregations, sharing reports on how we are doing. Perhaps most importantly, I also created a plan to thank and recognize individuals who participated and who hit certain milestones.

In 2012 we had 208 participating volunteers, and we exceeded our 2012 goal by processing 648,000 records. One thing that really helped was that we had a great project around which to rally: the Indexing of the 1940 US Census. That was a great way to get many of the volunteers fired up.

Do a good turn daily

Starting as a young eight-year-old boy, I began participating in Cub Scouts and then Boy Scouts. This time included many, many service projects and culminated in my own Eagle Scout project when I was sixteen. For my project, we collected food, clothes, and soft toys for a special needs school in Puerto Peñasco, Mexico. As an adult I have served as an assistant Explorer Post Advisor (think assistant scoutmaster for 16 to 18 year-old boys), an assistant Varsity Coach (think assistant scoutmaster but for 14 and 15 year-old boys). I am currently serving as a merit badge counselor for the Genealogy Merit Badge and as a Webelos Den Leader (ten year-old boys). I have also taken my three boys on many of the scout camp outs.

I grew up in a family of six kids, which in and of itself provides lots of opportunities for squabbles *and* service. I recall how my younger brother and I would squabble, one getting the other one mad until a chase would ensue; sometimes I was after him and sometimes vice-versa. Once when he was chasing me in fierce anger, I tripped and was hurt. He instantly changed from anger to concern for me and helped me up.

Jason Brimhall

Salt Lake City, UT, USA

MVP 2014 – Present

Category: Data Platform

Jason trains people on SQL Server. He has written several books and does a tremendous amount of blogging. He enjoys presenting at conferences and trade shows, and loves mentoring people. Jason also helps organize the massive SQL PASS Summit, where he selects speakers for the summit.

Jason coaches little league (basketball, football, and baseball), is a Cub Scout Den leader, and has been involved in scouting for 30 years. He enjoys helping out schools, primarily with their technical needs, but also with reading mentoring. He was an official volunteer French Translator for the 2002 Salt Lake Olympics.

Jason travelled a long road to earn his Bachelor's degree in Business Information Systems, oftentimes interrupting that time to support his family. In the end he not only graduated, but earned several honors.

Jason has *fun* wrangling developers and keeping them from committing what he calls "Crimes Against SQL."

Jason is always trying to learn more, dive deeper, and expand his horizons and expertise, all so that he can be better equipped to help others. His passion is clear in his motto regarding service to others: "Whatever it takes."

His passion is clear in his motto regarding service to others: "Whatever it takes."

Ben Zobrist – Committed Christian

Ben told me that he is "heavily involved in [his] home church, [and] home community – Nashville, TN – [as well as his] community bible church, [and as he is] originally from Eureka, IL, [he tries] to go back and do things there." According to a source cited in Wikipedia, he was a counselor in a Christian summer camp in Central Illinois called Camp of Champions USA (Piniat, 2009). Additionally, Ben participates in the aforementioned Show and Go Podcast aimed at helping younger minor league players and others getting started in baseball. And lest we forget, he has also been known to help older ladies disembark from aircraft.

Dale Murphy – Sportsman of the Year & Humanitarian Hall of Famer

On Dec 21, 1987, Sports Illustrated proclaimed Dale Murphy one of its Sportsmen/women/folk of the year (Deford, 1987). In 1995 the Boise, ID based Sports Humanitarian Hall of Fame inducted Murphy to honor his contributions to the world (World Sports Humanitarian Hall of Fame, n.d.). In 1985 he was awarded the Lou Gehrig Award for character and sportsmanship, and in 1991 the Bart Giamatti Community Service Award (Murphy, About Dale Murphy, n.d.).

A Mother's example

Dale began learning the value of service started at an early age. "One of the most striking memories of my childhood is my mother going to school every day as a volunteer to teach handicapped children… She could help someone, so she did. I was always taught that a meaningful life is just that" (Gammons, 1987).

Make a Wish, Write a Column

Despite the hectic schedule during baseball season, Murphy always made time for others, and during the offseason he increased his service hours. His activities vary wildly, from visiting children in the hospital, to raising money for the treatment of cystic fibrosis and other diseases, to serving as the chairman of a chapter of the Make-A-Wish Foundation, to encouraging kids to read (Gammons, 1987). He also wrote a column for the young readers of the Atlanta Journal and Constitution discussing "how to work with an umpire, how to deal with slumps in baseball and in life, how to avoid the problems of drugs. In lieu of payment, Dale [had] the newspaper make four-year scholarships available to deserving students" (Wolsey, 1985).

Who wants to wake up early while on vacation?

For two years during his offseason he also taught early morning (6:30 a.m.) religion classes every weekday to high school age youth (Gammons, 1987).

I Won't Cheat

After retiring from baseball, Dale has continued his amazing volunteer efforts. He served three years full time as a missionary for his church. He served on the Board of Governors at Operation Smile and the National Advisory Board for Operation Kids (Operation Kids now the offical charity of choice for Real Salt Lake, 2008). In 2006 Dale founded and ran the I Won't Cheat Foundation until about 2012. During that time, they offered a monthly $1,000 scholarship essay contest (Haws, Former Major League Baseball Player Dale Murphy Introduces Monthly Contest to Win a $1,000 Scholarship Award Through 'I Won't Cheat!' Foundation, 2008), formed partnerships with Little League Baseball, MLB, the NFL, and the NBA, and "reached more than 4 million children and had 50 events a year on character education" (Haws, Marty Haws, n.d.) .

Business value of giving back

Giving back should be done without expectation of return or reward; however, giving back can be good for the bottom line.

Brand Recognition

Giving back publicly can build your brand recognition. As your organization or team volunteers, raises money, or donates money, your marketing team will usually celebrate this. How can this apply to your personal brand as well?

Brand Polishing

This can also help polish your brand as you can involve your customers in your efforts. Some of your customer facing personnel in businesses with long term relationships can ask a customer to sponsor them in the 5k run. However, they do need to avoid being overbearing.

Attract and Retain Employees that care

Giving back can also help you attract and retain employees that care. In a case study of one consulting company on the eastern seaboard of the United States, Intellinet, Mark Seeley (company president) showed the connection between giving back and high-quality people. "Employees feel that they are working for more than a paycheck… That dedication to service bleeds into the type of service we provide for our clients… it's allowed us to attract a mission-based person," and "our customers almost invariably comment on the quality of people" (Garnett, 2013).

Networking

As you and your coworkers volunteer at larger events this can lead to intermingling of people and networking opportunities will abound.

"Successful corporate leaders understand promoting public opinions that are favorable to your company, boosting internal morale and improving the area you live in are all good reasons to make positive contributions to your community" (Boitnott, 2015).

I am not rich or famous, how can I give back?

The former President of Brigham Young University explained, "To worthy causes and needy people, we can give time if we don't have money, and we can give love when our time runs out" (Holland, 1996).

"We can give time if we don't have money,
and we can give love when our time runs out"
– Jeffery R Holland,
former President of Brigham Young University

Start in small ways and don't underestimate your impact. The slogan of the Boy Scouts of America, "Do a good turn daily," epitomizes this approach.

JustServe.org is a community service website open to all to sign up to volunteer or to look for volunteers. It has listings of opportunities across the United States of America.

If you have some programming skills, try Humanitarian Toolbox, an open source effort to solve technology problems related to emergency preparedness and disaster relief.

Schools are always in need of volunteers to read to struggling kids, to mentor kids, and to run programs like Art Masterpiece, or Junior Achievement.

Churches often have needs, as do cities and towns, Boys and Girls Club, Boy Scouts of America (and all of its brother and sister organizations throughout the world), Trail Life USA, Girl Scouts, and many more.

Feed My Starving Children has eight permanent food packing sites in four states, where volunteers come to pack nutritious, life-saving food "into bags which are then sealed, boxed, placed on pallets and shipped to our incredible partners working hard to reach the neediest children around the world" (Feed My Starving Children, n.d.).

Action Plan: How can I give back?

Where can I make a difference?

How can I make a difference?

How can I make a difference wisely? i.e. how can I avoid supporting a scam?

- Look for an organization that uses wise measurements.
    1. For Example, Feed My Starving Children has a map showing where they have shipped food, the date of the last shipment and how many meals have shipped to date.
- Look for signs of transparency.
    1. Do they make it easy to see their audited financial reports? For example, the Forever Young Foundation has their audited results right on their website.
    2. Do their executives make a reasonable amount of money?
        1. High enough to attract and retain talented leaders.
        2. Low enough that these executives aren't getting rich enough to buy their own islands.

Part IV How can I be an MVP in Life?

MVPs are so amazing, they do so well individually, they do so much to lift up their teams, and others outside of their arenas. How can mere mortals hope to achieve such heights?

Well, MVPs are human too. They weren't born outperforming everyone. They certainly don't have everything perfect. and they all must retire someday. What then?

Let's explore the human side of MVPs and see what can happen in your own life when you step up and be the MVP.

- <u>Chapter 8: Be the MVP</u>

Chapter 8: Be the MVP

Be an MVP – not a Rockstar

Dale Murphy – Author, Missionary, Restaurateur, Dad

Mike Halsey

Steve Nash – Family Man and Philanthropist

Sid the Kid Crosby – Still in the game

Steve Young – Hedge Fund Investor, Author, Philanthropist, Dad

Ben Zobrist – Dad and Future Pastor or Business Consultant?

Still just people

Hal Hostetler

Spark

Call to Action

Keeping in Touch

Be an MVP – not a Rockstar

The images conjured by the word MVP vs the images conjured by the word Rockstar present some interesting comparison and contrasts:

- They both play extremely well.
- They both tend to practice constantly.
- The MVP listens to the coach, whereas the Rockstar constantly fights with the coach and trashes the hotel room.
- The MVP displays their persistence as they work through injuries and challenges, whereas the Rockstar causes many of his or her own injuries through self-destructive behavior.
- While the MVP passes the ball, the Rockstar steals from other members of their own band.
- The MVP praises his teammates, but the Rockstar hogs the spotlight, excluding key members of the band.
- The MVP cares about the game and others, whereas the Rockstar only cares about the music and themselves.

Obviously, not all sports MVPs or Microsoft MVPs are as wonderful as those featured in this book. Even the MVPs that I have profiled have their flaws. Likewise, not all Rock Stars are as selfish as the stereotype portrayed above, and even the selfish ones have some redeeming characteristics. Sometimes the sports MVP behaves much more like the selfish Rockstar, and there are Rock stars that behave or have behaved much more like the MVPs I have highlighted. I want you to climb for the heights of the ideals of the MVP rather than stumble into the pitfalls of the typical Rockstar.

Dale Murphy – Author, Missionary, Restaurateur, Dad

 Betty Murphy, Dale's Mother, once commented on her son's potential, saying that "when he works with [his wife] to become another MVP – Most Valuable Parent – then he will really have achieved something" (Wolsey, 1985).

Lawrence Jordan, Dale's former Bishop (unpaid leader of his congregation) commented that "what the world doesn't know is that Dale Murphy is not only MVP in baseball, but in his personal life as well. He's not perfect, but his life is in high order" (Wolsey, 1985).

"When he works with [his wife] to become
another MVP – Most Valuable Parent – then
he will really have achieved something."
– Betty Murphy, mother of Dale Murphy

Dale responds to praise like this with genuine humility. "Believe me, I have many more faults than that. I don't want to give the impression that I am an almost perfect human being" (Wulf, 1983).

Restaurateur

In 2017, Dale opened a new restaurant called Murph's near the Braves new stadium in Atlanta, GA.

Missionary

Dale served a three-year mission for his church (supervising over 200 young missionaries, including one of my friends), and has written two books – all with the intent of helping and inspiring.

Author

His first book, <u>The Scouting Report on Professional Athletics</u>, takes a very baseball like approach to provide a scouting report teaching one how to watch out for the curves and fastballs of work/life balance as a pro athlete. He gives insight into picking agents, setting up your business affairs, giving back, and preparing for life after pro athletics.

Alarmed by the increase in poor behavior in youth athletes as they copied the poor examples of the Rockstar pro athletes, Dale wrote his second book, <u>The Scouting Report for Youth Athletics</u>. The book comes with a 50-page question and answer "insert which includes contributions from, among others, Peyton Manning, Dwyane Wade, Tom Glavine, and Danica Patrick," where they discuss the lessons they learned from youth sports and how they apply the lessons today." Concerned that youth might also follow the dangerous, high profile examples of steroid use, he also included "a physician-penned section about illegal performance-enhancing drug use in sports" (Dale Murphy, n.d.).

Speaking

Murphy speaks to many groups, and in 2015, Dale was recruited by the Forum on Character Education, put on by Character.org to deliver their keynote address in part as a result of have written his latest book. In their blog post announcing him as the keynote speaker, they noted that in his book on youth athletics he "promoted 'three primary responsibilities' for coaches… 'No. 1: Create a positive atmosphere in which players can achieve and learn.' 'No. 2: Teach proper fundamentals,' and 'No. 3: Demonstrate to each player that you care'" (Bauer, 2015).

Steve Nash – Family Man and Philanthropist

In Steve's farewell address he expressed his mixed emotions. "I will likely never play basketball again. It's bittersweet. I already miss the game deeply, but I'm also really excited to learn to do something else." He then pivoted to address "kids everywhere who have no idea what the future holds or how to take charge of their place in it." Steve made it clear that while thinking of his "career, I can't help but think of the kid with his ball, falling in love," and that he knows change is coming, especially a bigger focus on his family: "Lastly, Lola, Bella and Matteo, you're the center of my universe. All my focus and energy is here for you guys and moving forward, I couldn't think of anything more exciting or rewarding" (Nash, 2015).

I keep seeing Nash's charity efforts on Facebook, holding different events to raise money for his causes. Go Nash!

Sid the Kid Crosby – Still in the game

Sidney continues to serve as the Captain of the Pittsburgh Penguins and led the Penguins to the Stanley Cup (championship) in 2016 and again in 2017, winning the Playoff MVP award both years.

Mike Halsey

Sheffield, UK

MVP 2011 – Present

Category: Windows and

Devices for IT

An excited reader of Mike's first book nominated him to be an MVP. Mike received an email about his nomination, which was the first he had heard of the program. He filled out his response and forgot about it until the email announcing he had been selected to receive the award.

Mike answers questions on forums, writes lots and lots of books, and creates stellar videos (they are very well done and highly recommended). In fact, through his efforts to teach and mentor many other MVPs on methods and strategies for making good videos, he might be an MVP to many other MVPs. (Yes, it's his fault I started making videos, too, but the flaws are all my own.)

One of Mike's breaks occurred when Microsoft asked MVPs (because MVPs have more credibility than Microsoft employees) to travel the UK and help people understand why it was important to switch to Windows 7.

> A true explorer, Mike takes risks confronting new challenges. To improve himself, he constantly seeks out new training opportunities to boldly go where no MVP has gone before!

A true explorer, Mike takes risks confronting new challenges. To improve himself, he constantly seeks out new training opportunities to boldly go where no MVP has gone before!

https://mvp.microsoft.com/en-us/PublicProfile/4030748
https://www.linkedin.com/in/halseymike/
https://www.youtube.com/channel/UCkxtRni_WySua9CuOyr_K5Q
Mike: David's Book Reviews notes and videos on DavidPLundell.com

Steve Young – Hedge Fund Investor, Author, Philanthropist, Dad

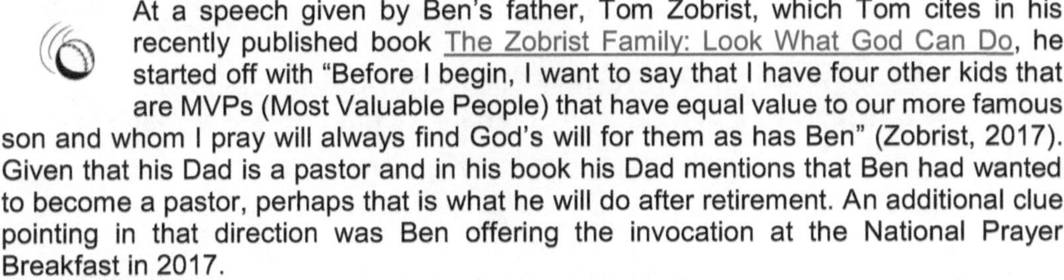

Steve Young has found life after football and is still trying to make those around him better. He is a founding partner in a venture capital firm, and he continues his philanthropy with the Forever Young Foundation. Most importantly, he devotes himself to his wife and children. In fact, the writing of his autobiography was an outgrowth of an effort to clear some things up for his children who heard various things on the playground. Steve also appears frequently as an analyst for ESPN.

Ben Zobrist – Dad and Future Pastor or Business Consultant?

At a speech given by Ben's father, Tom Zobrist, which Tom cites in his recently published book <u>The Zobrist Family: Look What God Can Do</u>, he started off with "Before I begin, I want to say that I have four other kids that are MVPs (Most Valuable People) that have equal value to our more famous son and whom I pray will always find God's will for them as has Ben" (Zobrist, 2017). Given that his Dad is a pastor and in his book his Dad mentions that Ben had wanted to become a pastor, perhaps that is what he will do after retirement. An additional clue pointing in that direction was Ben offering the invocation at the National Prayer Breakfast in 2017.

At the National Prayer Breakfast, Ben expressed great perspective. "Lord, You know that all I did was just hit a leather ball with a wooden stick and millions of people went nuts. But something much, much, more is happening here" (Zobrist, 2017).

> "Lord, You know that all I did was just hit a
> leather ball with a wooden stick and millions
> of people went nuts. But something much,
> much, more is happening here."
> – Ben Zobrist at the
> National Prayer Breakfast in 2017

In 2013 Ben also appeared as himself in a Christian film, called <u>Ring the Bell</u>. Perhaps film is also in his future (Weber, 2013).

In the meantime, Ben is still playing baseball for the Chicago Cubs and hopefully will do more of The Show and Go Podcast with his friends. Earlier in the book I commented that based on The Show and Go Podcast and my interview with him that I could see him as a business consultant or career coach to people in high stress roles.

Still just people

Despite all the amazing things that MVPs do, they are still just people and definitely aren't perfect. Dale Murphy once kicked a water cooler in the dugout (Associate Press, 1985). Steve Young hurled profanities at his head coach after getting benched (Tameta, 2009). Sid Crosby once saw an opposing player lose his glove and as he went to scoop it up, Sid pushed the glove away with his stick (Wyshynski, 2012). In 2018, Ben Zobrist was thrown out of a game after having a misunderstanding with an umpire. Steve Nash sadly went through a divorce. I am only too keenly aware of my own faults. Every MVP I know puts on their pants one leg at a time, unless they are sitting down, in which case they might try two legs at a time. more helpful than many my initial ones were.

Carol Wapshere, former Microsoft MVP, made huge contributions while she was still figuring out the technology by blogging about her journey.

In other words, there is hope for everyone. Many MVPs have achieved much while they are still trying to figure life out. One of my good friends, Carol Wapshere, former Microsoft MVP, made huge contributions while she was still figuring out the technology by blogging about her journey. Whereas, many of my initial blog posts were quite esoteric and were designed to show how smart I was. Consequently, I suspect her blog posts have been much

As a college freshman, I once missed out on an opportunity to help someone in need and I regretted it for months. One Saturday as I was cleaning out my truck I saw an old man, clearly indigent, going through our apartment dumpster looking for aluminum cans that he could take to the recycling center to collect a few cents for each. He wasn't asking for help; he was trying to help himself. Nonetheless, I felt within me a desire to help him by giving some food to him, but I wasn't done cleaning my truck, so I pushed the thought aside. As I looked up from time to time I saw him still there. Once I was finished with my truck, I looked up and he was gone. I ran over to the dumpster and looked in the alley, but to no avail. For months, I fervently hoped for a chance to see him again. The last day I was ever at that apartment I saw him again and immediately ran over to him, asked him to not go anywhere letting him know that I had something for him. I ran up the stairs to my apartment and returned with some fruit and cans of food, which the man happily accepted.

Hal Hostetler

Tucson, AZ USA

MVP 1996 – Present

Category: Outlook

Previous categories: Personal Operating Systems, Desktop Systems, XP, Windows Experience

Hal got his start with the Radio Shack Marble One (the TRS-80 computer, affectionately known as the "Trash 80"), which led him into Radio, Computers, and a long career in broadcasting at KVOA.

One day Hal had trouble getting the Outlook client to download email, so he went to the Microsoft News groups (now Answers.com) looking for help. While he couldn't find any answers for his issue, he *did* see others pleading for help that he was able to provide. He soon got hooked on answering questions, and in early 1997 MVP Sue Mosher (of slipstick.com fame) nominated him to be an MVP.

Over the years Hal has collected thank you notes from garbage collection personnel as well as heads of state and everyone in between, as he has answered questions on Collab365, Exchange launch events, TechEd (now MS Ignite), Facebook, Twitter, and Answers.com. He has presented at user groups in Tucson and other locations.

Some years ago, Hal and Russ Valentine (a cardiac surgeon and Microsoft MVP) became the gurus for Microsoft Fax.

Hal volunteers to take care of a two-way radio system, Cactus Intertie, and used to help out a religious station in Tucson as well. He still runs the monthly chapter meeting for the Ham Radio – Society of Broadcast Engineers (14205 2nd Sun of the month 2400 Zulu time).

Knee and back surgeries led Hal into a forced retirement; nevertheless, he keeps plugging away helping more and more people on the forums. He is grateful for the chances he has been given to help people at TechEd, as well as the opportunity to see the world.

https://mvp.microsoft.com/en-us/PublicProfile/5938
https://www.linkedin.com/in/hal-hostetler-514420a/
https://twitter.com/TVWizard

Spark

Inspiration is the spark by which we all seek to improve ourselves and the world around us. Paradoxically, we get the spark more often by doing than by waiting around. We all know of some good thing we can do. Sometimes, we wonder if it is the best thing to do. Often it won't be the best, but it just might be good enough and we each need to start somewhere. By doing good, we will be uplifted and inspired to better things. By doing better things, we will be filled with deep satisfaction and in turn lift our vision once more to do the best things.

Don't wait. Do something good right now. Send someone a short message of encouragement or say something nice to someone. Even better, do something nice for someone or make a committed plan to do it.

When we help others, we benefit too. Our perspective shifts, our problems don't seem as insurmountable, and we reawaken within us a capacity to do.

Call to Action

2 years in Venezuela

From 1994 to 1996, I lived in Venezuela as a missionary for my church. I didn't write this book to preach my religion to you, although it is a defining characteristic of who I am. The important thing to note is that after meeting, visiting, teaching, and serving the people of Venezuela, I came to care for them deeply.

Current Situation in Venezuela

As of March 2018, the facts on the ground are these: many people in Venezuela are having a hard time finding food and it is almost impossible to find medicine. Sending these to the country is fraught with peril. I have long felt powerless to help. It isn't safe to visit and sending the items that they need is difficult if not impossible.

I have kept in touch with some of the people I met during my time there. I offered to help one of my friends when she needed to buy her daughter glasses. For a variety of reasons, sending money to Venezuela can either be simple or it can be effective, but not both, and oftentimes neither. I did manage to help her get the seeing eye glasses.

How we might help

While speaking with another friend about the situation and my powerlessness, he related how our church has been trying to teach principles and skills related to self-sufficiency, and that in addition to that the people in Venezuela need to learn more technical skills to be able to start businesses. I felt inspired. I could finally envision a way to help. As a Microsoft MVP, I am considered one of the best experts in the world with certain technologies. I could teach Venezuelans over the Internet for free and help them learn skills that could help them start a business or get work from someone. I could inspire other MVPs to do the same. I could invite many others who have lived in Venezuela to help as well.

I called one of my good friends who was with me in Venezuela. He and his wife are experts in growing and making your own food and medicine (home remedies). It occurred to us that those are some of the most needed skills.

Lend us your skills, open your hearts, and spread the word! Let's help a nation of people to help themselves! Subscribe to the newsletter on DavidPLundell.com for more information.

I will cite one verse as a call to action: In the New Testament, James wrote an Epistle and in verse 27 of Chapter 1, he said this: "Pure religion and undefiled before God and the Father is this, To visit the fatherless and widows in their affliction."

I pledge to donate 25% of the net profits from this book to help defray the costs associated with this effort.

Keeping in Touch

Best wishes on your personal journey to becoming a sports MVP, a Microsoft MVP, or an MVP in Life. I would love to hear the stories of your journeys, your feedback, and your ideas. Please reach out to me at David@DavidPLundell.com

I offer a range of consulting and speaking services in

- IT (focused on Identity Management)
- Career Coaching (especially transitioning from technical to management)
- Business Leadership (setting the right culture for your team or organization, developing your vision)

If you feel the need to discuss more, or think I can be of assistance, please email me at: David@DavidPLundell.com

Acknowledgements

There are many who have helped me on my journey in life and in writing this book:

My wife – for enduring many hours of "What do you think of this, help me brainstorm that."

My kids – for giving up some time with me.

My editor, Levi Melton – for his encouragement, coaching and preserving my voice my while making this book better than it was before, including inspiring me with a key direction for the book!

Bill Gates – for founding Microsoft.

Microsoft – for founding the Microsoft MVP program.

MVP Program – for their encouragement.

My fellow MVPs – for being such amazing people that inspired me to write their stories – I could have picked another random set of MVPs and ended up with different stories that were just as wonderful.

My friend, Brad Turner – for nominating me to be an MVP.

My siblings – for enduring various rounds of, "How does this sound?"

My friends, associates, and internet friends – for all the feedback and encouragement.

My Book Cover designer, Laura Boyle – for going above and beyond to help my book have a beautiful face.

My clients – for trusting me with their identities.

My co-worker, Joe Zamora – who continually does a great job for our clients and stepped up when I needed time to grieve.

References

2003-04 Phoenix Suns Roster and Stats. (n.d.). Retrieved from Basketball Reference: https://www.basketball-reference.com/teams/PHO/2004.html

(2009). Retrieved from FanGraphs: https://www.fangraphs.com/leaders.aspx?pos=all&stats=bat&lg=all&qual=y&type=6&season=2009&month=0

AP. (2016, November 3). *Ben Zobrist named World Series MVP after 10th-inning RBI double*. Retrieved from ESPN: www.espn.com/mlb/story/_/id/17959237/2016-world-series-ben-zobrist-chicago-cubs-mvp-go-ahead-rbi-10th

Associate Press. (1985, March 31). Dale Murphy Is Again Soft Spoken and Affable. *Los Angeles Times*.

Associated Press. (2006, May 8). Nash named MVP again. *Los Angeles Times*.

Bailey, P. (2007). *Steve Nash: Most Valuable Player*. Moydart Press.

Baseball Reference. (n.d.). *Ben Zobrist*. Retrieved from Baseball Reference: https://www.baseball-reference.com/players/z/zobribe01.shtml

Basketball Reference. (n.d.). *Steve Nash*. Retrieved from Basketball Reference: https://www.basketball-reference.com/players/n/nashst01.html

Bauer, R. (2015, March 20). *Coaching for Character: Tips from Dale Murphy's Writing*. Retrieved from Character.Org: http://info.character.org/blog/-temporary-slug-cfa253ed-ce0c-4076-a9c5-fab139807b79

Becoming an MVP. (2015, July 3). Retrieved from Microsoft MVP: http://mvp.microsoft.com/en-us/becoming-an-mvp.aspx

Boitnott, J. (2015, January 27). *4 Ways Your Company Benefits From Giving Back*. Retrieved from Entrepreneur: https://www.entrepreneur.com/article/241983

Breech, J. (2013, October 25). *Flashback: Steve Young's 43-year, $40-million USFL Contract*. Retrieved September 13, 2018, from CBS Sports: https://www.cbssports.com/nfl/news/flashback-steve-youngs-43-year-40-million-usfl-contract/

Canadian Press. (2010, Mar 10). *Sidney Crosby*. Retrieved from Hockey News: www.thehockeynews.com/news/article/sidney-crosby-donates-20000-gold-medal-bonus-to-his-charitable-foundation

Chapman, G., & White, P. (2012). *The 5 Languages of Appreciation in Workplace*. Northfield Publishing.

Conley, C. (2016, November 3). *Zobrist, former Woodchuck, is MVP*. Retrieved from WSAU: wsau.com/news/articles/2016/nov/03/former-woodchuck-is-world-series-mvp/

Dale Murphy. (n.d.). Retrieved September 24, 2018, from Wikipedia: https://en.wikipedia.org/wiki/Dale_Murphy

Dale Murphy. (2018, March 21). Retrieved from Baseball Reference: https://www.baseball-reference.com/players/m/murphda05.shtml

Deford, F. (1987, December 21). A Little Lower Than the Angels. *Sports Illustrated*.

Demak, R. (1991, April 8). Mysterious Malady. *Sports Illustrated*.

Dillard, T. (2018, March 5). *Player & Coach Communication*. Retrieved from Show and Go Podcast: https://theshowandgo.podbean.com/e/player-coach-communication/

Feed My Starving Children. (n.d.). *Volunteer Info*. Retrieved from Feed My Starving Children: https://www.fmsc.org/get-involved/volunteer-info

Feschuk, D. &. (2014). *Steve Nash: The Unlikely Ascent of a Superstar*. Random House Canada.

Foran, C. (2005, November). The World according to Nash. *Toro Magazine*.

Forever Young Foundation -- About. (2018, March 20). Retrieved from Forever Young Foundation: foreveryoung.org/about/

Forever Young Foundation. (n.d.). *About Us*. Retrieved September 24, 2018, from Forever Young Foundation: http://foreveryoung.org/about

Forever Young Foundation. (n.d.). *Engage Now Africa*. Retrieved from Forever Young Foundation: http://foreveryoung.org/charities/africa/

Forever Young Foundation. (n.d.). *Forever Young Zones*. Retrieved September 24, 2018, from Forever Young Foundation: http://foreveryoung.org/charities/zone/

Fox Sports. (2013, October 25). *Young still raking in big USFL bucks?* Retrieved from Fox Sports: https://www.foxsports.com/nfl/story/report-steve-young-still-banking-big-bucks-from-usfl-contract-102513

Gammons, P. (1987, December 21). A Man Who Can't Say No: Dale Murphy. *Sports Illustrated*.

Garnett, L. (2013, December 13). *Why Giving Back is Good for Business*. Retrieved from Inc.: https://www.inc.com/laura-garnett/why-giving-back-is-good-for-business.html

Geracie, B. (1998, January 22). Hard working Nash becomes Suns' rising star. *San Jose Mercury News*.

Gladwell, M. (2015). *Hi, I'm Malcolm Gladwell, author of The Tipping Point, Blink, Outliers and--most recently--David and Goliath: Underdogs, Misfits and the Art of Battling Giants. Ask me anything!* Retrieved from Reddit: https://www.reddit.com/r/IAmA/comments/2740ct/hi_im_malcolm_gladwell_author_of_the_tipping/chx6ku3/

Hargreaves, J. (2013, September 5). Crosby discusses lengthy recovery road from concussions, safety of the game. *The Globe and Mail*.

Haws, M. (2008, April 17). *Former Major League Baseball Player Dale Murphy Introduces Monthly Contest to Win a $1,000 Scholarship Award Through 'I Won't Cheat!' Foundation*. Retrieved from Business Wire: https://www.businesswire.com/news/home/20080417005935/en/Major-League-Baseball-Player-Dale-Murphy-Introduces

Haws, M. (n.d.). *Marty Haws*. Retrieved from Social 5: https://university.social5.com/our_team/marty-haws/

Hockey Reference. (n.d.). *Sidney Crosby*. Retrieved from Hockey Reference: https://www.hockey-reference.com/players/c/crosbsi01.html

Holland, J. R. (1996, April). *A Handful of Meal and a Little Oil*. Retrieved from LDS Church General Conference: https://www.lds.org/general-conference/1996/04/a-handful-of-meal-and-a-little-oil?lang=eng

KSL. (2016, Oct 25). *tThe Doug Wright Show -- Steve Young Was Once Told He Couldn't Be the QB*. Retrieved from KSL: https://www.ksl.com/article/41980993/steve-young-was-once-told-he-couldnt-be-the-qb

Marin, C. (2011, September 25). *Crosby's a poster boy for more than just hockey*. Retrieved from Pros Give Back: http://prosgiveback.com/crosbys-a-poster-boy-for-more-than-just-hockey/

McCallum, J. (2006, January 30). Point Guard From Another Planet. *Sports Illustrated*, p. 9.

Murphy, N. (2011, July 27). *Getting Traded to the Phillies - The Rest of the Story*. Retrieved from Dale Murphy 3: https://dalemurphy.com/getting-traded-to-the-phillies-the-rest-of-the-story/

Murphy, N. (2011, August 14). *Thank you Bobby Cox!* Retrieved from Dale Murphy: https://dalemurphy.com/thank-you-bobby-cox/

Murphy, N. (n.d.). *About Dale Murphy*. Retrieved from Dale Murphy: https://dalemurphy.com/about/

Nash, S. (2015, March 21). *Life After Basketball*. Retrieved from The Players' Tribune: https://www.theplayerstribune.com/en-us/articles/steve-nash-retirement

NFL. (2016, Jan 25). *Super Bowl XXIX Recap: Chargers vs. 49ers | NFL*. Retrieved from YouTube: https://www.youtube.com/watch?v=pi1XDyrQJ8w&time_continue=144

NFL Network. (2015, March 10). Bill Walsh: A Football Life - The West Coast Offense. https://www.youtube.com/watch?v=X6mFQvZxX88.

NHL.com. (2018, June 20). *Mark Messier NHL Leadership Award Winners*. Retrieved September 24, 2018, from National Hockey League:

https://www.nhl.com/news/mark-messier-nhl-leadership-award-winners-complete-list/c-288172778

Olympic. (2004, April 11). *Leap of faith: Dick Fosbury on how a new jump style changed his sport forever*. Retrieved from Olypmic: https://www.olympic.org/news/leap-of-faith-dick-fosbury-on-how-a-new-jump-style-changed-his-sport-forever

Olympic Rewind. (2014, April 13). *Dick Fosbury Interview - Developing The Fosbury Flop*. Retrieved from YouTube: https://www.youtube.com/watch?v=gGqQXDkpgss

Operation Kids now the offical charity of choice for Real Salt Lake. (2008, April 1). Retrieved from http://blog.operationkids.org/2008/04/operation-kids-now-the-official-charity-of-choice-for-real-salt-lake/

Patterson, K., Grenny, J., McMillan, R., & Switzler, A. (2002). *Crucial Conversations*. McGraw-Hill.

Phoenix Suns at Dallas Mavericks Box Score, May 20, 2005. (n.d.). Retrieved from BasketBall Reference: https://www.basketball-reference.com/boxscores/200505200DAL.html

Piniat, E. (2009, June 25). *Former AIA Player Makes it to the "Big Leagues"*. Retrieved from Athletes in Action: https://web.archive.org/web/20110725023533/http://www.athletesinaction.org/news/post/Former-AIA-Player-Makes-it-to-the-e2809cBig-Leaguee2809d.aspx

Pro Football Reference. (n.d.). *Divisional Round - Chicago Bears at San Francisco 49ers - January 7th, 1995*. Retrieved from Pro Football Reference: https://www.pro-football-reference.com/boxscores/199501070sfo.htm

Pro Football Reference. (n.d.). *NFC Championship - Dallas Cowboys at San Francisco 49ers - January 15th, 1995*. Retrieved from Pro Football Reference: https://www.pro-football-reference.com/boxscores/199501150sfo.htm

Pro Football Reference. (n.d.). *Super Bowl XXIX - San Francisco 49ers vs. San Diego Chargers - January 29th, 1995*. Retrieved from Pro Football Reference: https://www.pro-football-reference.com/boxscores/199501290sdg.htm

Reevy, M. (2014, September 20). *The 10 highest scoring quarterback-receiver duos of all time*. Retrieved from Sports Cheat Sheet: https://www.cheatsheet.com/sports/the-10-highest-scoring-quarterback-receiver-duos-of-all-time.html/?a=viewall

Rossi, R. (2008, October 20). *Crosby not worried about puck*. Retrieved from Pittsburgh Tribune Live: https://triblive.com/x/pittsburghtrib/sports/s_594125.html

Schlossberg, D. (2010). *Marvelous Murphy: Too Good to Ignore*. Retrieved from SABR Society for American Baseball Research: http://sabr.org/research/marvelous-murphy-too-good-ignore

Sidney Crosby. (n.d.). Retrieved from Wikipedia: https://en.wikipedia.org/wiki/Sidney_Crosby

Sidney Crosby. (n.d.). Retrieved from Wikipedia: https://en.wikipedia.org/wiki/Sidney_Crosby

Smith, D. P. (2017, May 9). *Forever Young Foundation Board Meeting.* Retrieved from Forever Young Foundation: http://foreveryoung.org/wp-content/uploads/2015/08/FYF_Board_Minutes_2017.pdf

Staff Writer/Pittsburgh Penguins. (2011, July 7). *Crosby Foundation Supports Teen Lounge.* Retrieved from Penguins: https://www.nhl.com/penguins/news/crosby-foundation-supports-teen-lounge/c-568787

Stellino, V. (1990, December 12). Montana zooms from 5th to 1st in NFL salary race PRO FOOTBALL. *Baltimore Sun.* Retrieved September 13, 2018, from http://articles.baltimoresun.com/1990-12-12/sports/1990346110_1_million-montana-contract

Steve Nash. (2016, October 25). Retrieved from Wikipedia: https://en.wikipedia.org/wiki/Steve_Nash

Steve Nash Foundation -- What We Do. (2018, March 20). Retrieved from Steve Nash Foundation: https://stevenash.org/what-we-do/

Steve Nash Foundation. (n.d.). *BC Grants.* Retrieved from Steve Nash Foundation: https://stevenash.org/bc-grants/

Steve Nash Foundation. (n.d.). *Educare.* Retrieved from Steve Nash Foundation: https://stevenash.org/educare/

Steve Nash Foundation. (n.d.). *Reach.* Retrieved from Steve Nash Foundation: https://stevenash.org/reach/

Steve Nash Foundation. (n.d.). *Starting Five.* Retrieved from Steve Nash Foundation: https://stevenash.org/startingfive/

Steve Young BYU's All-American QB. (1984). Retrieved from Bigger Faster Stronger: http://www.biggerfasterstronger.com/uploads2/84_Jan_SteveYoung.pdf

Suzzane61. (2014, August 20). *My Nonprofit Reviews.* Retrieved from Great Nonprofits: https://greatnonprofits.org/users/profile/274381

Tameta, A. (2009, Septemeber 9). *Memories From the Glory Years: Steve Young's 1994 Tirade.* Retrieved from 49ers Webzone: https://www.49erswebzone.com/commentary/763-memories-glory-years-steve-youngs-1994-tirade/

ThePostGame Staff. (2013, October 25). *Despite New Reports, Steve Young Is Not Still Making Money From His Original USFL Contract .* Retrieved from ThePostGame: http://www.thepostgame.com/blog/dish/201310/steve-young-set-huge-payday-2014

Tuffaha, N. (2017, May 20). Sr Director at Microsoft. (D. Lundell, Interviewer)

VintageDawkins. (2017, April 17). *Steve Nash Full Highlights 2005 WCSF Game 6 at Mavs - 39 Pts, 12 Assists, 9 Rebs, CLUTCH!* Retrieved from YouTube: https://www.youtube.com/watch?time_continue=360&v=qvLDBdACoJM

Wagner, R., & Harter, J. (2014). *12: The Elements of Great Managing.* Gallup Press.

Weber, T. (Director). (2013). *Ring the Bell* [Motion Picture].

Wikipedia. (n.d.). *2004-2005 Phoenix Suns Season.* Retrieved from Wikipedia: https://en.wikipedia.org/wiki/2004%E2%80%9305_Phoenix_Suns_season

Wolsey, H. G. (1985, April). Dale Murphy -- MVP. *Ensign.*

World Sports Humanitarian Hall of Fame. (n.d.). *Dale Murphy -- Inductee.* Retrieved from World Sports Humanitarian Hall of Fame: https://web.archive.org/web/20110821074018/http://www.sportshumanitarian.com:80/inductees/dale_murphy.html

Wulf, S. (1983, July 4). Murphy's Law is Nice Guys Finish First. *Sports Illustrated.*

Wyshynski, G. (2012, April 15). *Sidney Crosby gets testy after Flyers win: 'I don't like any guy on their team'.* Retrieved from Yahoo! Sports: https://sports.yahoo.com/blogs/nhl-puck-daddy/sidney-crosby-gets-testy-flyers-win-don-t-025712917.html

Young, S. &. (2016). *QB: My Life Behind the Spiral.* Houghton Mifflin Harcourt.

Young, S. (2016). *QB: My Life Behind the Spiral.* Mariner Books.

Young, S. (2016, October 12). Steve Young Talks Separation Anxiety, Relationship with Joe Montana. (P. King, Interviewer) Sports Illustrated. Retrieved from https://www.si.com/mmqb/2016/10/12/steve-young-talks

Young, S. (2017, February 5). Steve Young's mental struggle off the playing field. (A. Keteyian, Interviewer) CBS News. Retrieved from https://www.cbsnews.com/news/steve-youngs-mental-struggle-off-the-playing-field/

Zielinski, D. (2015, February 20). *Why Social Recognition Matters.* Retrieved from Society For Human Resource Management: https://www.shrm.org/ResourcesAndTools/hr-topics/technology/Pages/Why-Social-Recognition-Matters.aspx

Zobrist, T. (2017). *The Zobrist Family: Look What God Can Do.* Tyndale House Publishers, Inc.. Kindle Edition. .

Index

About the Author

David Lundell

12-time Microsoft MVP

Striving to Be an MVP in Life

Founder of Identity Managed	Father of Four
Consulted for many Fortune 500	Married 21+ years
Team Builder	Youth Football Coach
Corporate Trainer & Career Coach	Scout Leader
Conference Speaker	Volunteered 10k+ Hours

David's love for technology and automating tasks has made him one of the world's top experts in Identity Management. As the founder of Identity Managed, David's small consulting firm delivers top notch IT Consulting to top enterprises around the globe, helping these business streamline operations and improve security and compliance in a more and more dangerous world.

David's latest book is **How to Be an MVP in Life: Lessons from Sports and Tech MVP's**. David, himself is a twelve-time Microsoft MVP. In his previous book FIM Best Practices he showed how to establish a solid foundation for Identity Management in the Microsoft world.

David has worked for over 20 years in Technology (mostly focused on Identity Management), consulted for many of the Fortune 500, authored two technical books, including the first book on Microsoft Identity Management, FIM Best Practices Vol 1, spoken at various conferences and for 12 years Microsoft has honored him as one of a select few worldwide Most Valuable Professionals(MVP) in Identity Management.